ECOLOGY INTO ECONOMICS WON'T GO

The notion that we can have sustainable economic growth is a delusion. Furthermore, the current attempts to solve our environmental problems through market-based incentives are as ineffective as a re-arrangement of the deckchairs on the Titanic. The culprit is the economic system itself, which acts against life and nature. The continuing transfer of resources from poor to rich countries, the burning of the rainforests, increasing third world poverty, spreading desertification, and the entirety of our environmental crisis can all be traced back directly to the nature of the economic system.

We have a stark choice to make: ecology, or economics. We cannot have both. Read this book and find out why.

STUART McBURNEY was born and brought up in Lancashire. He was educated at Chadderton Grammar School and West Kensington College, London, where he took an HND in Business Studies and Modern Languages. After many years working in the field of market planning, he turned to farming, and took a degree in agriculture at the University College of Wales, Aberystwyth. The writing of this book involved over five years' work, and he now intends to return to agriculture.

ECOLOGY
INTO ECONOMICS
WON'T GO

or LIFE IS NOT A CONCEPT

STUART McBURNEY

GREEN
BOOKS

First published in 1990 by
Green Books
Ford House, Hartland
Bideford, Devon EX39 6EE

Typeset by
Fine Line Publishing Services,
Witney, Oxon

Printed on recycled paper

Printed by Hartnolls
Victoria Square, Bodmin
Cornwall

British Library Cataloguing in Publication Data
McBurney, Stuart
Ecology into economics won't go, or, Life is not a concept.
1. Environment. Economic aspects
I. Title
304.2

ISBN 1-870098-28-5

Dedicated to Fergie, Mary, Mum and Dad.

With special thanks to Lao Tzu, Bob, Murray Bookchin, the North American Indians and all Aboriginal Peoples;

and in loving living:
  of Jimi Hendrix, for 'being',
  of John Lennon, and of his song 'Imagine'.

Acknowledgements

My most sincere thanks go to Jackie Smith and my wife Mary for the cartoons, and to Robert Whiteley for the illuminated capitals, the painting, and the photographs.

The publishers and I also wish to thank the following who have given permission for the use of copyright material, especially those who have been generous in waiving or reducing their fees. In the case of excerpts from *Touch the Earth* (ed. T.C. McLuhan, Abacus, 1971), I have made every effort to locate the various copyright-holders, and any further permissions received will be acknowledged in subsequent editions.

Fritjof Capra, for quotations from *The Turning Point* by Fritjof Capra. Copyright © 1982 by Fritjof Capra. Reprinted by permission of the author.

Cheshire Books for extracts from Murray Bookchin, *The Ecology of Freedom* (1982).

W.H. Freeman & Co. for the use of excerpts from *Agricultural Ecology* by G.W. Cox and M. D. Atkins, Copyright © 1979 by W.H. Freeman & Co. Used by permission.

Oxford University Press for material from World Commission on Environment and Development, *Our Common Future* (1987).

Penguin Books, for verses from Lao Tzu, *Tao Te Ching*, trans. by L.C. Lau (1963).

Saunders College Publishing: for excerpts from *Ecosystems, Energy and Population* by Jonathan Turk, Robert & Jane Witters, and Amos Turk, copyright © 1975 by Saunders College Publishing, a division of Holt Rinehart & Winston, Inc., reprinted by permission of the publisher.

Thorsons Publishing, for an extract from R. Norton-Taylor, *Whose Land Is It Anyway?* (1982).

UNCTAD, for material from the *Handbook of International Trade and Development* (1985).

The Worldwatch Institute for quotations from Lester Brown, *State of the World*, published by Norton, UK (1986).

Finally, I would like to acknowledge the influence of the following books not referred to in the text:

K. Dahlberg, *Beyond the Green Revolution*, Plenum, New York (1979).
E. Fromm, *To Have or To Be*, Abacus, UK (1976).
G. Leach, *Energy and Food Production*, I.P.C., USA (1976).
A. Watts, *Tao – The Watercourse Way*, Penguin, UK (1975).

Contents

Acknowledgements   vi
Preface   ix
Introduction   1

Chapter 1   Humankind's Attempt to Conceptualize   7

Cohesion – the essence of ecological existence   10
The '100 per cent' nature of experiencing   13
Time, space and ecological cohesion   15
Existence is sensible, and so too are we   17
Fergie in the looking glass   18
Our attempt to conceptualize ourselves   21
Our attempt to conceptualize things other than ourselves   25
Life is not a concept   29

Chapter 2   We Experience the Attempt to Conceptualize
             and its Consequences   31

The aeroplane   34
A totalitarian effect   36
The need to educate our children to conceptualize   37
Laws, which we attempt to enforce   40
The need for a God, a faith and a religion   40
The Fall, original sin – and my cat, Poubelle   41
The attempt to enumerate existence   42

Chapter 3   Today's Major Consequence:
             The Global Economic System   45

No ecologically meaningful basis for ownership   47
Living on enough is really disarming   66
The *more* ethic, and greed   68
Ownership necessitates exchange   71

A balanced exchange of resources   74
The development from balanced to unbalanced exchange of
   resources   77
From him that hath not ... shall be taken away   79
Ecological balance   85
Profit: a doctrine of imbalance   87
The middle ground ... is forbidden territory   90
'Profit-pull' and ecological sustainability   95
No ecologically meaningful basis for employment   100
Today's population explosion is caused by economics   106
Energy to our elbow   110
Time, rate and acceleration   112
Intuitive and conceptualized demand   119
Growth – or is it a growth?   126
Economic growth, investment and risk   130
High energy users   131
Energy is the first pollutant   140
Inflation – or is it 'inflammation'?   144
Unemployment   145
Industrialization   147
Specialization   149
Communications that keep us apart   154
Consumerism, the 'throw-away' society and vandalism   155
And this is how it works ...(a resumé)   156
Our assumption of separability   161
A global economic totalitarianism   163
Uniformity, diversity and ecological sustainability   168
Economics itself is the problem   172
Ecology into economics won't go   173
Attempting to live a concept of our lives   175
Paradise, lost?   183

Chapter 4   Intuitive Being   187

   Or better still ...   190

Preface

So far, the formal response to our newly-awakened concern for the environment has been parochial and superficial:
- petrol forecourts are being painted green, but our global over-use of fossil-fuel energy continues;
- toxic wastes are considered to be dangerous if dumped near human habitation, but safe if incinerated at sea;
- aerosols have become ozone-friendly, but consumerism sprints on unabashed;
- new, polluting industries are sprouting up, to monitor and clean-up old, polluting industries;
- global market forces run rampant, resulting in products which damage the Earth's atmosphere; but we are being told here in Britain that the self-same market forces are to be allowed to determine the rate and scale of our attempts to rectify the damage.

The framework within which we have to live our lives is being painted 'green', but it is still the same framework.

What makes this response so astoundingly inadequate is that it continues to propound the myth that we can go on using the world as if it is *separate* from us; that we are immune to the consequences of our actions; and that having now seriously injured the Earth's ecology, we can rectify the situation, without the process necessarily having to affect our lives in any fundamental way. This attitude, which assumes the separability of ourselves from the world we inhabit, is embodied in our current, global, economic system so that, for example, concern for the world's economic balance sheet is dealt with separately from concern for the world's ecological balance sheet. After all, ecology and economics are different subjects, aren't they?

But in reality all human economic activity obtains its every calorie of energy and its every gram of material from either the global ecosystem or the solar ecosystem; and ultimately, humankind is itself *a part of* the Earth's ecology. Acceptance of this fact demands that we do not continue to live our lives in the way we have been doing during our recent history.

Let me present a short analogy to highlight this latter point:

> *Homo economicus* is walking along a street in the City of London, carrying a briefcase which contains a compendium of world trade. His briefcase is very chic. Someone hands him a report on the state of the world's ecology, and on how he can clean up the mess. *Homo economicus* pops the report into his briefcase, and as he continues along the street, the briefcase appears to become even more chic; it takes on an attractive green tinge, and positively radiates a new-found prosperity.
>
> At this point however, *Homo economicus* remembers, as we have just done above, that he too is part of the world's ecology, so he includes himself in the new report and jumps into the briefcase.

The world's ecology is not something we can do things *to*, without our inevitably doing it to ourselves as well. As Arthur Miller recently observed, in reiterating sentiments previously expressed by Ibsen and Henry David Thoreau: 'Natures's ruin is a metaphor of man's self-betrayal.' And in just the same vein, we cannot put right the disruption we have caused the Earth's ecosystem, without its inevitably affecting our own lives.

An ecologically meaningful response to our current global predicament therefore necessarily involves us in an acknowledgement of humankind's essential *cohesion* with the Earth's ecology, and such an acknowledgement takes our current debate on the environment into a new realm and magnitude of thinking.

President Gorbachev exhibited an appreciation of this fact in his address to the United Nations in December 1988, when he propounded the notion that in future the totality of the consequences of humankind's activities would have to be taken into consideration, in determining how we are going to progress from this point in our evolution. More specifically, Mr. Gorbachev asserted that we had left behind the age of the zero-sum game, where the objective is to score points off one another:

> The formula of development 'at the expense of others' is on the way out. In the light of existing coalition, no genuine progress is possible at the expense of the rights and freedoms of individuals and nations, nor at the expense of nature.
>
> (The Guardian 9/12/88)

With this calibre of perception, we begin to move away from an economics-orientated management of both ourselves and of the world's resources, towards a recognition of the fact that *all* groupings of humankind must be adequately nourished and cared for, and that our provider, namely the Earth's ecosystem, must be allowed to display its inherent ecological sustainability.

But whence do we derive such an all-encompassing 'holistic appreciation' of our current predicament and of how we need to live life in the future?

For tens, and even hundreds of thousands of years, humankind has been attempting to live a 'conceptualized' version of its life. Nonetheless, today's philosophical debate still turns on the issue of whether we can in fact meaningfully conceptualize our own ecological existence; can we conceptualize the absolute Truth about our lives on Earth?

Thus for example, in his review of the recently published book *Contingency, Irony and Solidarity* by Richard Rorty (Professor of Humanities at the University of Virginia), Desmond Christy says the following:

> For centuries, priests, scientists and thinkers have gone in search of that philosophical grail – The Truth. But Richard Rorty believes that the truth about the Truth is that it only exists in the thoughts and words of those who search for it.
>
> (The Guardian 23/6/89)

Similarly, Walter Schwarz, in discussing Don Cupitt's new book entitled *Radicals, and the future of the Church* (1989) says:

> There is no truth, let alone absolute truth. No God 'out there', only God in our minds, ...
>
> (The Guardian 5/6/89)

However, what is apparently not questioned in such deliberations is whether we can actually 'conceptualize' in the first place?

In his memorable sentence 'Of what one cannot speak, one must be silent', Wittgenstein hinted that maybe we can't conceptualize everything. The significance of this is that if we can *not* conceptualize everything, and if we can *not* therefore conceptualize the absolute Truth, then it follows that we are not capable of conceptualizing an 'holistic appreciation' of our current predicament, nor of how we need to live in the future.

Ironically, however, it is in the acceptance of this very inability that I see the prospect of our actually achieving the holistic appreciation of our existence that we seek.

For is it not the case that we are currently, cautiously, feeling our way towards accepting that we do not need a conceptual framework any more within which to live our lives, because every single one of us is already an integral part of an intuitive, self-ordering reality?

Stuart McBurney
31/12/89

Introduction

'I've never done enough' said my father; and he was obviously very upset. I was nineteen years old, still at business college, and was trying to get my father to change the way he ran his garage business, so that he could perhaps work less hard and earn a bit more money. I was trying to help him, but he thought I was criticizing him.

It was 7.15 in the evening; my father had listened to 'The Archers' as he always did every night, and was getting his overalls on, ready to go back into the garage to 'Do a bit more', as he always said, every night. My dad was the nicest bloke I have ever met. What made me upset him? Why did I never seem to be satisfied with what he did? What was it that was apparently setting me against him?

As a result of my experience of life since that time and as a result of my having written this book, I have come to the conclusion that it is the *entirety* of the conceptualized, economic system and the *entirety* of the conceptualized, economic atmosphere of living, which humankind has created for itself over millenia, which is souring all our relationships, and which even soured my own relationship with my father. For it is, I believe, this conceptualized global economic system and atmosphere within which we live, which has attempted to introduce separation into what is ultimately an inseparable reality, and in so doing, has set person against person, nation against nation, and humankind against Nature. Indeed it has set humankind against all existence, when in reality we are part of it.

This book is my attempt to write down how I think this state of affairs has come about. Its creation has involved me in allowing

1

myself to acknowledge what my intuition has been telling me, and the excitement I have experienced whilst doing this has been reinforced by two certainties. Firstly, I have completely accepted the fact that I do not need formal qualifications before I can allow myself to express or act upon my intuitive feelings. In being ecological, I am inherently qualified to contribute my 'intuitions' on our current, global predicament, precisely because the world of which I am part *is* ecological; my credibility as a contributor emanates from the fact that I am ecological. Secondly, I have rejoiced in the knowledge that since every human being other than myself is also ecological, all other human beings must similarly have deep, intuitive feelings; that is, that each one of us inherently intuitive.

My sincere hope, therefore, is that what I have produced will eventually become just one droplet in a veritable flood of human, intuitive expression.

I started writing this book with two sets of intuitive feelings. First of all, I had a feeling of, and an inner appreciation of, the curves and proportions, the ebbs and the flows, the cycles and the fluxes, etc. which are intrinsic to the Nature of which I am a part, and which are therefore intrinsic to my own experiencing of existence:

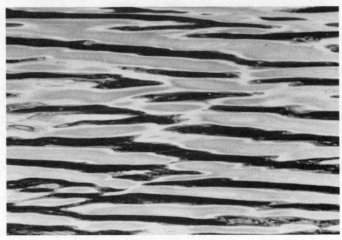

Water

2

Wood

Rock

Sky

Secondly, I had the intuitive feeling that much of human-kind's current experience of life, including my own, is being determined by economic imperatives and concepts which seem to *cut across* the functioning of the natural world, and hence seem to deny the full expression of those fluxes, curves and cycles, etc.:

Photo courtesy of US Department of
the Interior, Bureau of Reclamation

Cutting water

Cutting wood

Cutting rock

Cutting sky

4

This feeling was crystallized for me in 1978 when I came to the conclusion that the 'profit-motive' requires people to generate and maintain an *imbalance* in resource distribution, whilst in the natural world there is an ongoing tendency to engender *balance* amongst all things.

As a result of having had this perception, valid or otherwise, I began to mull over other economic concepts which also seemed to predominate in influencing the life we lead today: ownership, exchange, money, economic growth, specialization, etc. I wanted to detect what the basic characteristics of these concepts were, and then to see how these basic characteristics compared to those prevalent in the natural world. The approach proved fruitful, especially whenever I really let go and allowed myself to write down what I really *felt* about a certain economic concept and the effects it was having. I then realized that this discovery was not too surprising in itself. Being part of the natural, ecological world, I am imbued with ecological qualities that make me what I am. I am part of nature's balance, its rate, its cohesion and its diversity, for example. I don't *have* these qualities – they make me what I am.

Such qualities, among others, give me my capabilities, my capacities, my affinities, my energy and my limitations, and it is these that actually go to make up the entity that is me. I am, therefore, inherently sensitive to anything which attempts to impinge upon these qualities. I am my own ecological monitoring system.

Going back to the profit-motive once again, I realized that it was because my *own* sense of balance was being impinged upon that I had had the general perception that the profit-motive was a harbinger of relative imbalance in the wider world. I, like the rest of humankind, am daily exercized in trying to maintain an approximate balance in the living of my life. Therefore, when the profit-motive creates a situation of relative imbalance, as I believe it has, for example, in the global distribution of resources amongst members of the human family, I cannot help but be intrinsically aware of the fact.

This was a very exciting discovery for me, and as I looked at more of the economic concepts that mould so much of our current experience of life, I discovered that they all, in one way or another, impinge upon, or attempt to run contrary to, the universal ecological qualities that make me what I am. What I have written down, therefore, is an attempt to describe how this happens. In overall terms, it is an attempt to look at economics, ecologically.

As I continued my intuitive evaluation of the characteristics of economic concepts, one of their overall qualities was revealed to me. Not only do these concepts have an interdependence and a logical relationship, but also, one economic concept often seems to lead to the emergence of another. For example, the 'ownership' of resources inevitably requires the mechanism of 'exchange', and the exchange of resources creates the context in which 'profit-making' can evolve. In short, the order in which they might have been conceptualized began to emerge.

The introduction of a chronological element into my analysis drew the focus of my attention back in time to a consideration not only of how today's economic concepts might have arisen, but also of how humankind might have made its initial attempt to conceptualize.

The overall result of my endeavours includes, therefore, both an intuitively ecological evaluation of humankind's current economic lifestyle and an intuitively ecological evaluation of humankind's current conceptualized existence – the one having led to the other.

Ultimately, and although of necessity conceptualized, this book represents for me a sincere celebration of my ecological nature. In addition, since the ecological qualities that make me what I am are the ecological qualities that make all people what they are, and all existence what it is, this book is also a celebration of the ecological nature of all existence. Throughout, I have simply been referring myself to my intuition and to my ecological qualities. Anyone can do it.

Chapter One

Humankind's Attempt to Conceptualize

SOME HUMAN BEINGS write books, but most plants and animals don't. The reason for this apparent difference is that over the last few million years, the branch of hominids which we now refer to as *Homo sapiens* has made the attempt to conceptualize its own existence and can therefore write about it; whilst as far as we know plants and animals have either not attempted to do so, or have not tried as hard as we have.

This difference is, I believe, a difference in degree, in spite of the fact that humankind would like to think itself *absolutely* different in terms of its ability to conceptualize and think; and this very wish epitomizes the essential characteristic of our attempt to conceptualize and of our attempt to create a conceptualized existence. For in this endeavour we have assumed that we *are* different, that we are *separate from,* or are marked out from, plants and other animals, as well as from our Earthly context. However, since we are, in ecological reality, *part of* an absolutely *cohesive* ecological existence, this would appear to be a rather vain aspiration.

In the introductory sections of this book, therefore, I shall attempt to depict the cohesive nature of the existence of which humankind is a part, and then against this backcloth I shall present my assertion that our attempt to conceptualize has involved us in assuming that we are, in fact, separable from Nature.

Cohesion – the Essence of Ecological Existence

A relatively small proportion of the atoms of the Universe cohere to form the hand with which I am holding this pen and writing these words. The ballpoint of my pen is in contact with the paper on which I am writing, and when it is not directly so, it still 'coheres' with the paper via the atoms of oxygen and nitrogen, etc. in the atmosphere. The process of writing in which I am engaged is a manifestation of the synchronized functioning of my body's muscles, its nervous system and its primary sensibilities. The whole thing is a 'coherent' process.

In just the same way, but on a larger scale, my hand coheres with all the atoms that form this Earth and our galaxy because of the cohesiveness of the energy of which all are an expression. Similarly, as a single manifestation of the Universe's one flow of energy, our galaxy – the Milky Way – coheres with all the other galaxies in the Universe. Thus, for example, at a local Astronomy Group meeting recently, I was able to see the Andromeda Nebula, a near-neighbour galaxy, thanks to the light energy which joins me to it, and which had taken the trouble to travel for two million years, just to dump itself into the 4.5-inch telescope into which I was peering. From atomic to inter-galactic, the Universe of which we are a part is cohesive.

'Water, hill and tree' (painting by Robert Whiteley)

Aboriginal people have always sensed this quality. For example, Hin - mah - too - yah - lat - kekh (thunder - travelling - to - loftier - heights) of the Nez Perce Indians of North America said:

> The Earth and myself are of one mind. The measure of the land and the measure of our bodies are the same.
>
> *(Touch the Earth*, 1971, ed. T.C. McLuhan).

Similarly, in a *National Geographic* article (Vol. 173, no.2, February 1988) about the Gagudju, a small group of Australian Aborigines of the Northern Territory, we are told by the article's writer, Stanley Breeden:

> To understand the Gagudju is to understand their Dreamtime – to us a very complex concept, to the Gagudju a simple one that explains the cohesion and interdependence of all living things. 'Dreaming' and 'Dreamtime' are direct translations from the Aboriginal words, but in fact, have little to do with dreams as we know them. Dreamtime refers to the beginnings of life and its continuation into the future.

Photo by Belinca Wright © National Geographical Society

The late Silas Roberts, an Aboriginal leader close to the Gagudju, explained it this way: 'Aboriginals have a special connection with everything that is natural.... We see all things as part of us. All the things on Earth we see as part human.'

And again: 'In all these things,' Neidje (a Gagudju elder) stressed, 'all living things are as one.' He said: 'Earth our mother, eagle our cousin. Tree, he is pumping our blood. Grass is growing. And water. And we are all one.'

He added that when the ancestral beings had completed their creation, they told the people: 'Now we have done these things, you make sure they remain like this for all time. You must not change anything.' Thus the people were charged with the custodianship of the land and all living things. It is what the Gagudju call: 'Looking after the country.' The Dreamtime then, is the cohesive force that keeps man and his environment in harmony.

Looking at nature's cohesion from a scientific viewpoint we can state that the Earth's myriad ecosystems cohere and harmonize with one another. Thus, in a *Guardian* article dated 13 November 1987, Anthony Tucker reported that an independent British Scientist, Dr Jim Lovelock, together with the US National Oceanic and Atmospheric Administration's Marine Environment Laboratory in Seattle and Washington University's Department of Atmospheric Sciences, had begun to unravel the ecological interconnectedness between the oceanic production of algae and oceanic cloud formation:

For handy biochemical reasons, most species of phyto-plankton in the oceans excrete a substance called dimethylsulphide, known as DMS for short. DMS escapes readily from the sea into the atmosphere where it reacts to form a continuously produced mass of fine particles (aerosol) of a 'non-sea-salt sulphate', which can be readily identified. Research has shown that these particles are dominant in the air over the oceans and, in recent studies, that they are also the dominant – perhaps even exclusive – nucleating particles in oceanic clouds. The latest studies clinch the relationship between sunlight, aerosol production and cloud formation.

Thus we can see that components of our environment that appear to function separately, in fact cohere and interact to create a self-balancing, self-regulating whole. Indeed it is this calibre of ecological interlinking that allows us to refer to the entirety of the Earth as being *one* cohesive ecosystem. (See, for example *Gaia: a New Look at Life on Earth*, 1979, 1987, by J.E. Lovelock.)

The '100 per cent' Nature of Experiencing

The process whereby a human being experiences things involves the five primary senses of sight, hearing, touch, taste and smell, plus what we might call our 'intuitive sensibility', which enables us to appreciate such composite sensations as apprehension, fear, joy, contentment and anger, etc., together with specific feelings of, for example, *balance*, the *rate* at which events occur, and the infinite *diversity* of our world. It might seem, in the first instance, that each of these six senses would contribute an equal proportion, i.e. about 17 per cent each, to the overall process of our experiencing, but somehow it doesn't seem to work like that.

If we consider a blind man, the sum of the stimuli he senses from the world around him is certainly reduced by his blindness, but the actual experiencing achieved by each of his remaining senses is still 100 per cent. If he experiences anger when he bumps into a car left parked over the curb of the pavement, his experiencing of anger is 100 per cent; it is not, shall we say, 83 per cent because he is blind. Similarly, if he smells a meal which is on the table in front of him, his experience of smelling is still 100 per cent.

We also find that where any one of these six senses is impaired in some way, then the actual experiencing by that impaired sense is still 100 per cent for the person involved. Consider a partially deaf lady with, shall we say, a 55 per cent hearing capability. When she hears the muffled and very quiet noises her hearing picks up, her experiencing of those sounds is still, for her, 100 per cent. The sounds she *does* hear constitute the *entirety* of her hearing experience, and she is only said to have a 55 per cent experience of hearing with reference to some externally determined criterion of 100 per cent. Somehow, we just don't seem to be able to experience at anything less than 100 per cent.

13

Similarly, the phenomena and occurrences which are the things we experience – these themselves give out 100 per cent of that which they are. For example, let us consider the coloration of a plum. In terms of light energy, a plum gives off, at any one time, a specific spectrum of wavelengths that accords with, and is a manifestation of, the coloration of the plum. The plum gives off, in terms of its coloration, the entirety of that which it *is*.

In addition to this, it would appear that the phenomena we experience are as they are, in the moment we experience them, as a result of everything else in the Universe being as it is, at that moment, and also as a result of all evolution having been as it has been, up to that moment.

Consider, for example, the quality of the noise coming from a jet airliner's engines as it flies overhead. The noise will result, amongst many other things, from the types of metals used in their construction. These metals will be the result of the state of technology in the aerospace industry, the availability of ready energy for the extraction, processing and manufacture of such metals, the current composition of the Earth's metal deposits, which, over geological time, will have been influenced by the levels of incoming solar radiation and by the temperatures and pressures at play at the Earth's surface; these in turn will have been influenced by the mean distance of the Earth from the Sun, our solar system's position in relation to the galaxy as a whole, and so on.

All these factors, as they have evolved to date, together with countless billions more, influence the quality and characteristics of the sound I hear from the jet airliner's engines. (This phenomenon is recognised in, for example, climatology, where it is referred to as 'the butterfly effect', and is an acknowledgment of the fact that the slightest occurrence on one side of the Earth [even a butterfly flapping its wings] can influence global weather patterns.)

It is on the basis of this type of reasoning that I assert that what we experience, we experience as a result of *everything* on Earth and in the Universe being as it is at that moment; which in turn is a result of everything having evolved in the way that

14

it has evolved, up to that moment. The experiencing of our every 'now' results from everything that 'is', and from everything that ever 'has been'.

This means, I believe, that the experiencing of our existence is indeed a 100 per cent process, and this feels to me to flow from the ecological fact that absolutely everything in the Universe *coheres* with absolutely everything else. Thus in existing, and in being a part of an absolutely cohesive existence, we experience – indeed we can only experience – the absolute entirety of everything that *is* the universe.

Time, Space and Ecological Cohesion

We can derive yet another appreciation of the absolute completeness and cohesion of our experience of existence by briefly considering the twin notions of 'time' and 'space'.

In terms of time, I only ever experience my existence *now*. In addition we can note that the 'now' I am experiencing here, as I write these words, is happening at the same time around the world and, indeed, throughout the Universe. The 'now' every human being experiences, and which every component of our ecological Universe experiences, is the same 'now' in the instant that it is happening. 'Now' happens simultaneously, everywhere, and hence we can say that 'now' is 'temporally cohesive'.

And 'now' is to time, as 'here' is to space. The only place in which I do my experiencing is *here*. This is the same for all human beings and for all components of ecological existence. What is more, all the 'heres' in which we all do our experiencing are spatially linked to one another. Consequently we can say that all 'heres' are 'spatially cohesive', just as all 'nows' are 'temporally cohesive'.

In terms of experiencing, therefore, there is only one 'now' and only one 'here'. This is because in terms of experiencing there are no such things as time and distance. My experiencing only ever happens now; therefore, if I am experiencing, it is always 'now', and hence 'now' is timeless. Similarly, my experiencing only ever happens 'here'; therefore, if I am experiencing, I am always 'here', and hence 'here' is without distance. What is more, in terms of

15

experiencing, my 'now' only ever happens 'here', and therefore I can reasonably say that they are one.

You Can't Get Away From It

There is only 'now', it's true to say,
but since it's always 'now', don't worry, it won't go away.
For example, if now at nine o'clock I say, 'See you all at ten',
by the time I do see you, it's 'now' again.

There is only 'here', it's true to say,
but since 'here' is everywhere, don't worry, it won't go away.
There's a 'here' waiting for you, wherever you go,
but if you do ever manage to dodge it, please let me know.

You see, 'here' is where your 'now' is happening,
the two are closely knit;
they seem to be together all the time,
you can't get away from it.

Harry Snodgrass Junior (1912)

Thus, whether we think at the level of atoms or galaxies; whether we study the functioning of the Earth's ecosystem; whether we consider the fact that we experience everything that 'is', and everything that ever 'has been' in every instant of our lives; or whether we acknowledge that we only ever experience our existence in our 'here' and our 'now', we can reasonably conclude that the process of our experiencing is, indeed, a 100 per cent, absolutely cohesive process. We are part of, what a good friend of mine once perceptively called, the *'immediacy'* of existence.

What is life? It is the flash of a firefly in the night.
It is the breath of a buffalo in the winter time.
It is the little shadow which runs across the grass
and loses itself in the Sunset.

(Spoken by Crowfoot of the
Blackfoot Indians of Alberta, Canada
From Touch the Earth, 1971, ed. T.C. McLuhan)

Existence Is Sensible, And So Too Are We

Ultimately, humankind, and all the components of evolution on Earth and in the Universe, are the infinitely variable manifestations of the Universe's energy; and the essence of that energy is its cohesiveness. In the fact that energy is our 'being', and hence in being energy, humankind coheres with all the energy that is everything else in the Universe. The surge of the energy that is us, and therefore the pulse of all human 'being', can do nothing other than go with the pulse of all energy, and hence the very fact of our existence means we are 'sensible of' the pulsing of all energy in the Universe.

This is because the vast flood of energy that is the Universe is itself a vast 'sensibility'. It cannot be anything else, because all its energy coheres, interflows and interpulses. Thus the flow, the surge and the flux of any part of the Universe's energy moves, pushes, draws and bends the flow of all other energy in the Universe. Energy cannot flow and flux *without* influencing and moving all other energy, nor without its movement being 'sensed' by all other energy, since to move something is to be 'sensed' by it.

For example, a surge of energy in a distant galaxy can be sensed and manifested as a swirl of energy in our own galaxy, which in turn can influence the conditions in our own solar system, influencing the pattern of solar flares on the surface of our own Sun. Such flares can subsequently move, affect and thereby be sensed by the ions in our Earth's own atmosphere, and an era of favourable ionic conditions on Earth, together with an era of favourable weather patterns, can in turn fuel a surge in vegetative growth and in animal populations here on Earth. Thus, a surge of energy out in the galaxies can find expression in, and hence can 'be sensed by', animal populations here on Earth. Thanks to its endless cohesion, thanks to its infinite interactivity, energy's very movement *is* a 'sensibility'.

Energy, and hence existence, is 'sensibility'. Existence and sensibility are synonymous terms, and thus in being a part of the Universe's energy and its existence, humankind can be nothing other than a 'sensibility' itself.

17

This sensibility which we *are*, this sensibility which, in existing, any one of us cannot *not* be, is, I believe, composed of our primary senses and, as we mentioned earlier, our intuitive sense. Our primary and intuitive sensing of things is the flowing of the energy we are; it is a manifestation of the sensibility we are. Everybody's primary and intuitive sensibility is everybody's bit of the vast sensibility that *is* existence. Our abilities to see, smell, touch, taste and hear, and our intuitive propensities to, for example,

- balance the various components of our lives,
- pace the rate of our living,
- seek diversity of experience,
- ensure a sufficiency in essential things, and
- be a part of, that is cohere with, all that is happening around us,

and our composite intuitive sensations of, for example, joy, sadness, anger, pity, excitement, etc. – all these forms of sensing and many more go to make up the overall sensibility that *is* our experience of living.

Existence is sensible, and our sensibility is our existence.

Fergie in the Looking Glass

However, the long-term human attempt to conceptualize our existence has involved us, I believe, in an attempt to *separate* ourselves from the flowing of the primary and intuitive sensibilities that make up our experiencing of existence. In attempting to conceptualize both ourselves and all that is around us, we have effectively tried to take one step back from ourselves and from the things that make up our environment; we have tried to make ourselves *aware* of our own, and their, existence.

This thought occurred to me one day as a result of a chance observation that I made of our son, Fergie. On 28 September 1984 Fergie, then nine months old, leaned forward towards a mirror and kissed his own image. My mother-in-law, in whose house we were living at the time, thought it amazing that he had kissed himself *on the lips*; and so did I for a few seconds, until I saw the inevitability of it. There was something in this incident that really made me smile, and I scribbled down some thoughts on it:

Fergie kissing his own lips in the mirror. Fergie is Fergie; his image is *not* Fergie, and Fergie, in trying to experience his image, is trying to kiss himself – self-perpetuating impossibility.

Fergie sees himself in a mirror and thinks: 'I can see myself – therefore I exist', but in fact Fergie is existing without a mirror image.

If we attempt to conceive of ourselves, as humankind has apparently done, we have immediately entered into a sort of cycle of effort which simply 'comes round on itself'. It is unending and we can spend our lives 'conceptualizing' rather than 'living'. Similarly, Fergie sees himself (a visual circuit) and kisses his own lips in the mirror (a physical circuit). He could go on looking at himself and kissing himself all his life, rather than kissing others and living amongst others! It's self-perpetuating, and makes a circuit which apparently attempts to be separate from the rest of 'living' and 'being'.

As Fergie is kissing the mirror, he is almost cutting himself off, in terms of his real interaction with the world, during the time he's

kissing himself, just as I cut myself off from my living context when I refer myself to my 'thoughts'. Referring myself to my conceptualized thought is a circuit within myself, whereas simply feeling my 'feelings' is an opening-up and a communicating outwards and inwards to the one flow of which we are all a part.

What really amused me about Fergie's actions was the fact that his real lips kissed his image's lips. His lips didn't kiss his image's shoulder, nor its forehead, nor its nose, they just kissed his image's lips – and of course that's all they could do. The action represented an absolute 'coming-back on itself'; a precise 'coming-back to the same place'. This made me feel that Fergie was effectively trying to 'loop back' on the experience he was already experiencing; on the experience that was him, 'being'. It looked as though he was trying to experience a 'second take' of himself. I also sensed that while he was looking into the mirror, the ongoing process of his 'being' had, in a certain sense, been effectively subordinated for a few seconds. In effect, his 'experiencing' had had to stop for a short time, whilst he 'observed himself experiencing'. In turn, this made me feel as though he had effectively been trying to *separate* himself from the ongoing process of his 'being', whilst he had been trying to observe himself being.

This episode reminded me of several attempts I had made as a young person to really *relish*, and to really *make myself aware of*, exciting and special moments in my own life. Thus, for example, as the early morning of Bonfire Day dawned, grey and cool, and often damp, I remember trying to 'stop' myself; I remember trying to breathe in and brace myself, in an attempt to really realize that 'it', this special event was actually happening:

> Now, here I am breathing in the cool, damp morning air, I'm smelling the stale old wood we've collected, I'm hearing the starlings on the rooftops. I'm here; I've been waiting for Bonfire Morning for so long, and now it's happening and I must really realize it's happening and enjoy it.

But this always seemed a very difficult thing to achieve. I never seemed to quite get hold of my excitement; there didn't seem to be anything to get hold *of*, and yet it was all happening in front of

20

me. It always felt as though it was just happening and I was just happening with it.

In trying to realize what I was feeling, in trying *to be aware* that I was experiencing, smelling and seeing something special, something exciting; in trying to really grip what I was experiencing at that moment, I felt as though I was trying to 'loop back' on what I was involved in; that I was trying to jump outside of myself so that I could see and feel 'me' from outside, experiencing the excitement of the moment.

> *But it was always slippery*
> *silvery*
> *thin as air;*
> *transparent,*
> *happening, but not quite there.*

In retrospect I feel that what I was trying to do then, and what I observed our son Fergie trying to do, is exactly the same as that which all humankind has been trying to do for hundreds of thousands of years. We have been trying to 'loop back' on, and thereby *separate ourselves from*, the very process of our experiencing, in order to 'conceptualize' our existence.

Our Attempt to Conceptualize Ourselves

For a long time now humankind has been trying to make itself aware that it *is existing*; it has been trying to make itself aware that it is seeing, smelling and hearing things, etc., rather than simply seeing, smelling and hearing things. It has been trying to become *aware* of its own existence. But for some reason this has proved to be an intrinsically difficult thing for us to do.

Why? Why was it not possible for Fergie to experience his own existence with the use of a mirror? Why was it so difficult for me to really realize and relish the excitement that I was feeling on Bonfire Morning? Why is it so difficult for us to really get a grip on our experiencing and our sensing, in the instant in which we are experiencing and sensing?

The reason, I believe, as was discussed at the start of the book, is that the process of experiencing our existence – that

21

is, the 'sensibility' that constitutes our existing and our experiencing – is absolutely *cohesive*. 'I', that is, me 'being', is my contribution to the Universe's expression of its absolute cohesion. My experiencing, and hence my sensing, is my part of the flowing of the Universe's infinitely cohesive energy, and therefore 'I' cannot experience me 'being', from anywhere else. I cannot *separate* myself from my existence, in order to observe myself existing.

As the world-famous Edwardian un-philosopher, Harry Snodgrass Senior said, in 1910:

' It's difficult to put your finger on 'being', because it <u>is</u> your finger.'

Since all my sensibilities constitute what I *am*, I can't send any of them over 'there' to monitor me happening 'here', because *I* would have gone with them. *I* wouldn't be 'here' any more, to be monitored. And yet this is precisely what our attempt to make ourselves *aware* of our existence has involved us in trying to do. This 'separation' is what humankind has required of itself in its continuing attempt to conceptualize its own existence.

Let's take a look at the implications this attempt would have for our primary senses of sight, smell, taste, touch and hearing. First of all, the sense organs would have to extend outwards, and then turn round, so that they could touch, taste, listen, smell and look back at us. This would allow them to sense our experiencing 'here', but from over 'there'.

However, since our primary sense organs would still be attached to our body they would not be able to see, hear, smell, taste or touch those specific points on our body from which they had extended themselves. Consequently, the primary sensings they would relay back to us would be *incomplete*. This is very significant because, as we discussed earlier, the process of our ecological experiencing, the process of our 'sensing', and also the very essence of any thing we sense and experience; all these things are '100 per cent'. Thus, for something to exist and be a part of our 100 per cent existence and similarly for something to be sensed and experienced by us, it has to be '100 per cent' itself.

Consequently, as part of our attempt to make a 'concept' of ourselves *exist*, we will need to ensure that the sensings our primary sense organs send back to us are similarly 100 per cent. However, they are not. They are, at best, 99 per cent and to make these sensings 100 per cent as we require them to be, each primary sense organ would have to become completely detached and *separated* from its host body. Only then would each sense organ be able to sense the entirety of the 'being' from which it had come – *including the point to which it had previously been attached*.

However, as we have already said, we are part of an absolutely cohesive ecological existence. The human body and all its components are a part of existence's absolutely *cohesive* flow of energy. Therefore, it is impossible to separate, in this instance, the primary sense organs from their host body.

This means that the host body can never present an absolutely final, outer surface to the primary sense organs for them to sense. As a result, the *sensing* of that host body or 'being' by the primary sense organs can never be 100 per cent, as is required for it to *exist* as part of the 100 per cent ecological existence of which we are a part. That is, the sensing of 'self' by the would-be human conceptualizer is always *less* than the

100 per cent required for the 'concept of self' to *exist* as part of our 100 per cent ecological existence.

What is more, I can back up this assertion by reiterating what I said earlier, about the nature of the very process of 'sensing', which constitutes my ecological existence. My 'sensibility', that is the sum total of my sensing, is absolutely everything there is of my experience of living. My sensing *is* the process of my existing. My sensing capacity is everything that is 'me', and I can only sense, and hence exist, to the extent of that capacity. Ultimately, therefore, and for each instant in time that I exist, that is all the sensing I can achieve; I cannot achieve an *additional* dose of sensing in any of the moments through which I exist.

Therefore, to the extent that my attempt to conceptualize myself involves me in trying to achieve a quantity of sensing that is *over and above* the sensing that is the totality of 'me', in any instant of my existence – I can't do it.

Consequently, we can reasonably conclude, I believe, that in the ecologically cohesive reality of which we are a part, humankind cannot conceptualize itself in an ecologically meaningful way. We can also say that the concept of 'self' does not exist.

Our Attempt To Conceptualize Things Other Than Ourselves

Up to this point in our discussions we have concentrated on humankind's long-term attempts to conceptualize 'self', and have revealed that this would appear to be an ecologically impossible thing for us to do. If we now consider our attempt to conceptualize things other than ourselves we will find, I believe, that this too is ecologically impossible.

The spectacle of the eyes (sorry about that), the ears, the nose, the fingers and the tongue of a human being extended out from, and separated from, and ultimately turned back upon the host body to which they belong, is admittedly rather far-fetched. Therefore, to present a slightly less bizarre illustration, and this time one which concerns humankind's attempt to conceptualize the things that are all around it, rather than itself, let us consider the 'spectacle' of the men who went to the Moon.

Here was a situation in which the astronauts, one would have thought, would have had a remarkable opportunity to observe the entirety of the 'thing' from which they had flown; namely, planet Earth. One would have thought that they would have been able to sense or to view the absolutely defined, final, outside edge of the Earth, and hence would have been able to create a 100 per cent, complete, and therefore ecologically meaningful concept of it.

However, for them to have been able to do this, they would have needed to have been completely and absolutely *separated* from Earth in terms of energy, so that they could 'view' the absolute entirety of the energy that constitutes Earth. But in ecological reality, the Moon astronauts were still in contact with the energy that *is* planet Earth, as a result, for example, of the light energy which flowed between themselves and the Earth.

CHADDERTON

Therefore, in being in visual contact with the Earth, and thus in having to sense it ultimately with their own primary sense organs, they were still linked to the Earth; they were *part of* that which they wanted to conceptualize.

> *On a sunny afternoon in 1910, Harry Snodgrass Senior said whimsically: 'From an ecological point of view, there isn't one'; and in so saying, showed that he too had fully appreciated this fundamental point.*

So the supposed concept the astronauts no doubt felt they had of planet Earth was, in fact, incomplete and deficient.

Humankind's attempt to achieve a 100 per cent observation of the things that are in its environment, in order to conceptualize them, ultimately involves it in obtaining an observation of itself, because in an ecologically cohesive world humankind is *part of* those things. It is therefore at *this* point that its attempt always founders, since, as we said earlier, humankind cannot separate itself from itself, to observe itself. Its *sensing* is all there is of its existence for each moment that it exists, and therefore it

26

cannot sense *additionally* the sensing that is the totality of its existence.

In an existence formed of absolutely cohesive energy, one 'thing' cannot sense another 'thing' because neither can exist as a discrete entity.

A 'beautiful woman' does not 'sense' a 'beautiful tree'; rather they are both *sensible of* one another because both are part of the one *sensibility* that is all existence. Their *sensing* of one another occurs as a result of the flowing of the absolutely cohesive energy that forms *both* of them.

In exactly the same way, and as we said earlier, 'I' can't sense 'myself'. Since a portion of the Universe's vast sensibility constitutes that which is me, I don't sense myself; my sensing *is me*. I am already part of an existence that *is* a sensibility, and therefore in simply existing, I sense. Consequently, there is no need for me to try to get a 100 per cent sensing of 'me'.

27

But this is precisely what humankind is trying to do, in its attempt to conceptualize its own existence and all that is around it. An attemptedly conceptualizing humankind would have itself *sense again* its *already sensible* existence.

And the Lord God planted a garden in Eden; and there he put the man whom he had formed. And out of the ground made the Lord God to grow every tree that is pleasant to the sight, and good for food; the tree of life also in the midst of the garden, and the tree of knowledge of good and evil....

And the Lord God took the man, and put him into the garden of Eden, to dress it and to keep it. And the Lord God commanded the man, saying, Of every tree of the garden thou mayest freely eat: But of the tree of the knowledge of good and evil, thou shalt not eat of it: for in the day that thou eatest thereof thou shalt surely die...

And the Lord God caused a deep sleep to fall upon Adam, and he slept: and he took one of his ribs, and closed up the flesh instead thereof: and the rib which the Lord God had taken from Man, made he a woman. and brought her unto the man.

And they were both naked, the man and his wife, and were not ashamed.

Now the serpent was more subtil than any beast of the field which the Lord God had made. And he said unto the woman, Yea, hath God said, Ye shall not eat of every tree of the garden?...

And when the woman saw that the tree [of knowledge] was good for food, and that it was pleasant to the eyes, and a tree to be desired to make one wise, she took of the fruit thereof, and did eat, and gave also unto her husband with her; and he did eat.
And the eyes of them both were opened, and they knew that they were naked;...

(from Genesis 2 and 3)

Life is not a Concept

Therefore, we can reasonably conclude by saying that:

Humankind cannot 'conceptualize',

nor can it make existence into a 'concept',

because the essence of ecological existence

is *cohesion*;

whilst the essence of humankind's attempt to 'conceptualize'

is assumed *separability*.

We can never make our attempted conceptualizing, nor our attempted concepts, into the 100 per cent things we would like them to be, and hence they can never become a part of our ecological existence.

From this it follows that 'concepts' do not exist.

As Harry Snodgrass Senior repeatedly said:

'You see, life is not a concept.'

Chapter Two

We Experience the Attempt to Conceptualize and its Consequences

N EVERTHELESS, THERE IS ample evidence all around us of a supposedly 'conceptualized' living of life. How can this possibly be the case if humankind can not 'conceptualize'? I would suggest that nowadays, our experience of existence is predominantly being influenced, not by 'conceptualization', not by 'concepts', but rather by the *attempt* to conceptualize and the *consequences* of that attempt. I would also maintain that these factors affect our experience of existence specifically because our attempt to conceptualize has failed.

As I said earlier, humankind's attempt to conceptualize has involved it in an attempt to separate itself from, and to 'get outside' the existence it would like to conceptualize, but because we are part of an absolutely cohesive ecological reality, we have never managed to achieve this. Therefore, our attempt to conceptualize has never, shall we say, managed to 'leave' existence; it is still 'in here with us' in this existence, and as a result, we experience both the *attempt* and the *consequences* of making that attempt.

The *attempt* to conceptualize and the *consequences* of that attempt exist as part of our 100 per cent ecological existence; they are 100 per cent phenomena, and it is as a result of this that we experience them.

Just as a paradoxical aside, it is interesting to note that humankind's attempt to conceptualize has had to fail (to separate itself from existence) for it to exist. Had the attempt to conceptualize (and to separate itself from existence) succeeded, then the resultant conceptualization would have been 'outside' of existence, and it would, therefore, have been impossible to experience it.

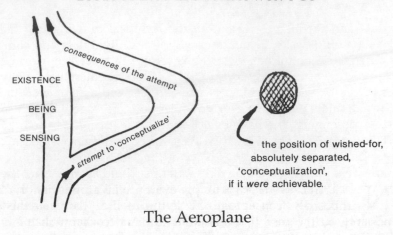

EXISTENCE

BEING

SENSING

consequences of the attempt

attempt to 'conceptualize'

the position of wished-for,
absolutely separated,
'conceptualization',
if it *were* achievable.

The Aeroplane

Today, all around the globe – on the land, on the oceans, and in the Earth's atmosphere – are to be seen the *consequences* of humankind's attempt to conceptualize: the notion of our being 'within' an earthly environment, concepts of 'components' in that environment, the employment of ourselves, our fellows and of components of the environment as instruments and tools to undertake 'conceptualization's' will, the products we manufacture, the use we make of stored sources of energy, the secondary results of all those activities, our institutions, protocols and hierarchies and so on. These consequences *do* exist and can be experienced in absolute, ecological terms. In existing, in occurring and in being experienced, these consequences are 'ecological'.

Let us consider a recent consequence of humankind's attempt to conceptualize; let us look again at the phenomenon of the jet airliner. One has just flown, five miles high, across the blue sky outside my window. How can such a phenomenon be a 100 per cent existent *consequence* of humankind's attempt to conceptualize, and yet be a 'concept' which, as we have just asserted, does *not* exist?

Let us first consider what we think might constitute the concept of the jet airliner. The concept we have of a jet airliner might be said to involve a metal vehicle which is propelled by a fuel-consuming jet-engine, and is designed to carry human passengers over continental and intercontinental distances. We could

34

then add to this description *all* the technical drawings, *all* the engineering-design evaluations, *all* the test flight data and computerized monitorings of in-flight service in existence from all over the world. We could put all this data together, in as many hangars as was necessary to take it; we could assemble *all* the airline pilots who have ever flown jet airliners, together with *all* the passengers who have ever flown in them, and get them all talking on the topic, and then we could say: 'Listen to that lot; that's what the concept of a jet airliner is'. And as far as is humanly possible, we'd be right. But this would *not* represent the ecological entirety of the total impact the jet airliner has had, or is having, on the Earth's ecosystem and indeed on the Universe's ecosystem. It would *not* represent the entirety of what we actually *experience* as the consequence of humankind's attempted conceptualization of a jet airliner.

Together with the global ecosystem, indeed together with the entire Universal ecosystem, we experience the absolute 100 per cent entirety of the *consequence* known as a jet airliner. Together with the ecosystem, we experience not only the fact that a jet airliner is a flying machine which can carry people from one spot on the globe to another. We also experience:

- noise pollution (resulting from the industries that manufacture jet-engine components as well as the operation of the engines themselves);
- atmospheric and potential climatic disturbance;
- psychological disruption of family units and communities, created by the human separation which results from 'easy' long-distance travel;
- specialization;
- profits for some, resulting from airliner manufacture and operation; loss for others, resulting from an imbalanced concentration in the use of the world's resources;
- heat pollution of the globe's atmosphere as a result of excessive CO_2 production by jet engines;
- the provision of ecologically superfluous speed; and
- the creation of an ecologically high risk-factor in flying five miles high, etc.

35

This list is obviously brief in the extreme, but what I am simply trying to indicate is that the *consequence* known as a jet airliner has an effect on millions of components in our ecosystem, and that since humankind is linked to *every one* of those components in being a part of that cohesive ecosystem, then the existence and functioning of jet airliners will, in any ecologically extensive summary, affect us in billions of ways.

We do not just experience a metal machine flying in the sky, carrying human beings, we experience *much, much more* than that, because the experienced ecological consequences of the jet airliner are much, much more than the concept; infinitely more, in fact, because the consequences exist, whilst the concept does not.

To summarize my argument up to this point, therefore, I would say that over a long period of time, humankind has been making the attempt to conceptualize; but since this involves us in assuming that things are separable in what is, in ecological reality, a cohesive world, we have never been able to do this. Nonetheless, we *have* been making the *attempt* to conceptualize, and this has had *consequences*, which we are experiencing today.

A Totalitarian Effect

This realization is large enough in its own right, but when we consider the extent to which humankind's current experience of ecological reality is affected by our attempt to conceptualize, the scale of this influence can be seen to be remarkable. I think it would be reasonable to claim that all of the developed world and increasingly large proportions of the developing world function under the *totalitarianism* of the consequences of our attempt to conceptualize and of our attempt to lead a conceptualized existence.

However, humankind's basic, ecological *sensing* capabilities and its *intuition* have not been killed by this totalitarianism; rather they have been extensively stifled, 'crusted-over' or subjugated by the consequences of the attempt to impose a conceptual totalitarianism. Underneath, human beings are still 100 per cent experiencing, intuitive, ecological components of an ecological existence. Nonetheless, the consequences of our manic attempt to create the uncreatable, and to experience the inexperiencable, are very substantially influencing humankind's actual, intuitive, ecological existence. I shall describe some examples of these consequences in the following sections.

The Need to *Educate* Our Children to Conceptualize

On education, the *Tao Te Ching*, a collection of ancient Chinese wisdom, has the following to say:

> *When the best student hears about The Way*
> *He practices it assiduously;*
> *When the average student hears about The Way*
> *It seems to him one moment there, and gone the next;*
> *When the worst student hears about The Way*
> *He laughs out loud.*
> *If he did not laugh*
> *It would be unworthy of being The Way.*

Tao Te Ching by Lao Tzu

On initial reading, this doesn't seem to make much sense – or at least it didn't when I first read it. But if you re-read it, bearing in mind that we already *are* what we need to be, and therefore that study and scholarship are unnecessary, then we begin to see that the student who 'laughs out loud' on reading the Tao, realizes that he or she does not *need* to study it. It's a complete waste of time and effort because he already *is* what the studies are trying to teach him to be.

From birth, all human beings are furnished with all the primary and intuitive sensibilities that are required to ensure our ecological survival, contentment and sustainability. Thus, conceptualization has to propound the myth that trying to teach children to conceptualize is *essential*, because the *attempt* to conceptualize is all there is of it. Conceptualization can never be part of our ecological existence or being, only the attempt to make it so. Hence, the attempt includes the eulogization of scholarship.

In being totally conceptualized, today's formal education can be said to be a part of humankind's apparatus for perpetuating its attempt to conceptualize, and for perpetuating its attempt to subjugate its own intuitive being. Children are born with their intuitive sensibility fully functional. They are bursting with intuition and spontaneity; their experiencing of existence is not cluttered with concept; they live intuitively in their 'here and now'; hence their ability to see straight through the imposed crust of conceptualization that is all about them in the adult world.

Children, and beneath our supposedly conceptualized crusts, we adults too, *are* all we need to be. As we have already discussed, all of humankind, all ecological evolution, the Earth, our solar system, etc. are all manifestations of the flowing of the Universe's energy. Everything is of that energy, and is imbued with the curves and the fluxes that characterize its flowing. These characteristics make existence, and as part of it, all humankind, what it is. We don't need to be taught our characteristics, nor do we need to be informed about our qualities – we *are* them.

To draw an analogy, a landscape's contours, its qualities and its characteristics, are brought out by its inevitable, ecological, unconceptualized, un-self-realised interaction with wind, water, temperature, etc. Why then, do we *teach* our children their qualities and capabilities, when their *real* qualities and characteristics are inherent in their 'being', and will be brought out and developed in the process of simply existing?

> And they brought young children to him, that he should touch them: and his disciples rebuked those that brought them. But when Jesus saw it, he was much displeased, and said unto them: 'Suffer the little children to come unto me, and forbid them not: for of such is the kingdom of God. Verily I say unto you, Whosoever shall not receive the kingdom of God as a little child, he shall not enter therein.' And he took them up in his arms, put his hands upon them, and blessed them.
>
> (Gospel According to St Mark 10: 13 – 16)

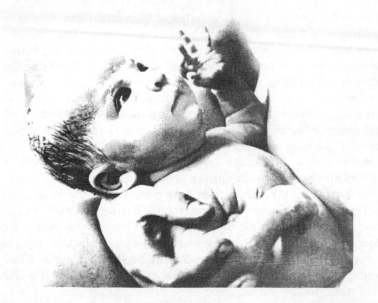

Laws, which we Attempt to Enforce

If the lifestyle we have today were intuitive and ecological, and did not involve us in a conceptualized attempt to instil, for example, separation into an inherently cohesive world, if it did not involve us in attempts to introduce imbalance into a self-balancing Nature, acceleration into a paced ecosystem and uniformity into a diverse reality, then of itself that lifestyle would harmonize and be 'at one' with our ecological existence.

But humankind's current, global lifestyle is *not* intuitive and ecological – it is conceptualized and economic. Since this lifestyle involves us in an attempt to contravene the ecological parameters and qualities that make us what we are, rather than flow with them, we are having to *force* its dictates onto our ecological lives. Laws, I believe, are simply part of the apparatus we have tried to conceptualize in order to do this. They form part of the equipment for forcing a conceptual lifestyle onto an intuitive humankind.

It is for this reason that there needs to be a thing called law-enforcement; whereas an ecological, intuitive living of life needs no enforcement – it *is* what we *are*.

The Need for a *God*, a Faith and a Religion

As I have said, humankind, in attempting to conceptualize, had to accept the premise that it could *separate* itself from its Earthly environment, and indeed, from its own experience of existence. However, once having got itself out into this supposedly detached, supposedly conceptualizing realm, the premise of its separability has, I believe, become a source of worry to a still intuitive, ecological humankind. Consequently, solace has been sought in a conceptualized solution. Humankind has conceptualized a god, who might still be able to keep us *in touch with* the existence we assume we have left behind. Subsequently, we have conceptualized having faith in that god.

The paradox is, however, that in being concepts, both the concept of god and the concept of faith are themselves imbued

40

with the assumption of separability they were intended to bridge. Thus in reality, more separation was being offered as the antidote to separation. And the result has been that it hasn't worked. No concept, no matter how fervently believed in, can bring us back into the existence we feel we have separated ourselves from, because *all* concepts assume that we *are* separated from that existence.

However, this assertion need not be a cause for worry. Though we believe we have separated ourselves from our existence and have, in this way, enabled ourselves to conceptualize, the reality is that we have never done either of these things. In the ecologically cohesive reality of which we are a part, there is no such separation possible – ever. Thus, we have no need for any vehicle, nor any solution, whether conceptualized god or conceptualized faith, to bring us back into existence, because we have never succeeded in getting out of existence.

And to reinforce this assertion, but for a moment still utilizing the religious concept of god, I can say the following: For me, the term 'god', is synonymous with the term 'all Creation', and therefore, since humankind is part of Creation, then we are all part of what is referred to as 'god'. This is what Jesus meant, I believe, when he said: 'I am the son of God.' We are *all* the sons and daughters of god, in that we are *all* the sons and daughters of ecological Creation.

The Fall, Original Sin – and my Cat, Poubelle

The 'Fall' in the Bible is synonymous with 'eating from the tree of knowledge', and I believe that this is a symbolic reference to humankind's attempt to conceptualize; I believe that the human attempt to conceptualize was the Fall. And having once fallen we have been blighted, generation upon generation, with the original sin of having fallen. Thus the need to be baptized, generation after generation, is perpetuated; and even after baptism, according to the Church, we are still inherently sinners, so that for us, a state of grace is always *somewhere else*.

41

But, as already stated, in ecological reality we never did manage to conceptualize. Therefore we never 'fell', the original sin was never perpetrated, and far from being a sinner, I am part of an ecological existence that is not only in a state of eternal Grace, it *is* eternal Grace.

Having said that, however, we *have attempted* to conceptualize and hence we *have attempted* to fall from grace, whilst most of the animal kingdom doesn't seem to have made the effort.

Some two years ago I observed what was for me a delightful example of this fact. Whilst writing a section of this book in my mother-in-law's garden shed, I looked up to see our cat, Poubelle (the French for 'pedal bin' rather than 'dustbin', because we kept treading on her), gracefully walking along the narrow edge of an opened cold-frame panel. Poubelle was not thinking: 'I might fall to the left' or 'I might fall to the right'. She wasn't thinking at all, she was just walking along the narrow edge of the panel – in perfect Grace.

The Attempt to *Enumerate* Existence

As we have established, the assumption of separability is the premise upon which humankind's attempt to conceptualize is based, and perhaps one of *the* most fundamental and all-pervasive consequences of that attempt is that all the supposed concepts that are assumed to have resulted, are themselves imbued with this self-same assumption of separability.

This applies to our attempt at quantitative, as well as qualitative conceptualization. Therefore, on examination we find that our attempt to *enumerate* existence is itself characterised by the assumption that any 'one' unit of a resource or phenomenon can be completely separated from, and hence identified as distinct from, any other unit of that resource or phenomenon. However, in an ecologically cohesive world, no 'one' supposed unit of anything is completely separable from its context, either in terms of the atoms that form it and its context, or in terms of the energy that *is* that unit and its context. Consequently, no item can lend itself to being identified as 'one' of anything.

On a larger scale, I can reasonably claim that since I am definitely experiencing an existence at the moment, and that since the existence of which I am a part is absolutely cohesive, then there must only be 'one' such existence. However, such certainty is inappropriate. How can I determine, from inside, where this 'one' cohesive existence finishes? And even if I could, what is then outside this existence's 'outer surface'?

I am driven to conclude therefore, that such an absolute definition is not ecologically possible and hence that the concept of 'one' of anything can not be created in an ecologically meaningful way.

Similarly, the concepts of two, three, four, etc., all assume that any phenomenon or resource can itself be separated to give two, three or more components, when again, such separation is not possible in our cohesive ecological reality.

And most fundamental of all, mathematics is said to be based on 'zero'. But what is zero, other than an assumption of nothing, of a gap or indeed, of separation? Zero is the mathematical equivalent of attempted conceptualization's qualitative assumption of separability:

+2
+1   Zero is the mathematically assumed gap between
 0   positive and negative, but in an ecologically cohe-
-1   sive reality, no such gap exists.
-2

Chapter 3

Today's Major Consequence: The Global Economic System

AS I HAVE SAID, the most fundamental consequence of humankind's continuing attempt to conceptualize is that all the
supposed concepts that result are themselves imbued with the
assumption of separability that underpins that attempt. Thus, if
we now examine an omnipotent and ubiquitous consequence of
humankind's current attempt to lead a conceptualized existence –
that is, today's global economic system – and specifically, if we
examine the concept of ownership which forms the basis of that
system, we find that the whole of today's economic edifice is built
upon the self-same assumption of separability. In this instance of
it, it is assumed that humankind can be separated from the
ecological, Earthly resource-base, of which, in reality, it is a part.

No Ecologically Meaningful Basis for *Ownership*

In this section I hope to achieve two things. Firstly, I should like to
put forward a hypothesis as to how the attempt might have been
made to create the concept of ownership; and secondly, I should
like to consider whether the supposed concept of ownership is
ecologically meaningful. But to start with, I should like to restate,
though in a slightly different way, the assertion that humankind
is part of an absolute cohesive ecological reality.

As a human being, I am in continual receipt of elements from
my habitat, mainly in the form of food, that go to make up my
physical body and to power my physical and sensory functioning. I also continually give elements back to my immediate
surroundings, for further use elsewhere in the habitat. After
physical death, of course, even the elements making up my
body are returned to the ground and hence go back into the

global resource-pool. Thus, in an absolute and physical sense I am connected to, and made up of, elements that emanate from my immediate environment. Without these elements I would not function, nor would I exist.

In a spiritual and psychological sense as well, we are all part of our surroundings, in that we feed off and contribute to the spiritual and psychological quality and vitality of our environment, at all times. In this way we are all part of an unbroken physical – psychological continuum, here on Earth.

Indigenous peoples had, and indeed still have, a profound and inherent appreciation of this fact. For example here, in a speech made around 1900 by Chief Standing Bear, reference is made to the Lakota tribe and their affinity with the natural environment:

The Lakota was a True Naturist – A Lover of Nature

He loved the earth and all things of the earth, the attachment growing with age. The old people came literally to love the soil and they sat or reclined on the ground with a feeling of being close to a mothering power. It was good for the skin to touch the earth and the old people liked to remove their moccasins and walk with bare feet on the sacred earth. Their tipis were built upon the earth and their altars were made of earth. The birds that flew in the air came to rest upon the earth and it was the final abiding place of all things that lived and grew. The soil was soothing, strengthening, cleansing and healing.

That is why the old Indian still sits upon the earth instead of propping himself up and away from its life-giving forces. For him, to sit or lie upon the ground is to be able to think more deeply and to feel more keenly; he can see more clearly into the mysteries of life and come closer in kinship to other lives about him.

Kinship with all creatures of the earth, sky and water was a real and active principle. For the animal and bird world there existed a brotherly feeling that kept the Lakota safe among them and so close did some of the Lakotas come to their feathered and furred friends that in true brotherhood they spoke a common tongue.

The old Lakota was wise. He knew that man's heart away from nature becomes hard; he knew that lack of respect for

48

growing, living things soon led to lack of respect for humans too.
So he kept his youth close to its softening influence.

(From *Touch the Earth*, 1971, ed. T. C. McLuhan)

However, in large part it would appear that today's conceptualizing humankind has forgotten that it is a part of Nature's absolute cohesion, and perhaps as a consequence it has sought, over the millenia, to 'own' the greater part of our ecosystem's accessible resources. It is against this backcloth that I should like to consider the question: How has the attempt been made to create the concept of ownership?

To hypothesize an answer to this question, I think it might be expedient for us to turn our minds back between one and one-and-a half million years, and to allow ourselves to consider how the then relatively sparse population, known as *Homo erectus*, might have related to its habitat. The human population at that time was sufficiently light to have ensured that every human being had a sufficiency of resources available to him or her. This was simply because where essential resources were not available, there was little or no human habitation. In physical terms the situation was as straightforward as that.

The other major factor which characterized the human population at that time was that it was 'un-self-realized'; that is, it had not attempted to develop any concept of 'self' (See, for example, *Human Origins*, 1982, by R. E. Leakey). However, at some point in its evolution, humankind began its attempt to conceptualize, and to become aware of 'self' and then of its actions and interactions with phenomena in its environment. It was only consequent upon this development that humankind was afforded the opportunity, firstly to make decisions about and to control its own actions, and secondly to reach out and attempt to manipulate the things that existed in its environment.

Thus with the attempt to conceptualize established, and with awareness of its actions developing, humankind felt itself ready to react 'knowingly' to its predicament, should the need arise. If, therefore, we now consider *Homo erectus* in a region in which there was a given supply of essential resources, capable of supporting a given size of human population over long spans of time, then whenever the human population density increased past the point where all the *unforced* plentitude of a given habitat was being fully consumed, we can hypothesize that one of two possible processes occurred: (a) either the human community *accepted* intuitively the need to keep its demand for resources *within* the unforced plentitude of resources from that region, or (b) it tried to *manipulate* its habitat knowingly, to increase the rate of supply of those resources, thereby allowing its numbers to increase.

Let us consider the second possibility first: In this hypothesized situation we have human beings who have attempted to manipulate their environment, hoping to enhance the output of resources so that it would support a larger human population. Such a development must have taken generations, indeed millennia, to have occurred, and in terms of its immediate effect, it must have felt like a healthy and creative course of action.

However, when viewed from the point of view of the ecological criteria and capacities, limitations and amplitudes intrinsic within that region's ecosystem, such manipulation, though absolutely marginal at that stage, nonetheless represented the *forcing* of an hitherto unforced output of resources. It represented the initial transgression of that habitat's ecological integrity.

> Because they are an integral part of Nature and the land, because they *are* the land, Aboriginal people can not understand why anyone would want to alter or destroy it – that would amount to killing the life-force. As one of them said: 'White man got no Dreaming. Him got 'nother way... him got road belong himself.' To the Aborigines it is a road contrary to nature and leads to eventual destruction.
>
> (From *National Geographic*, vol. 173, no. 2, p 278)
> from an article by Stanley Breeden

No matter how marginally, such manipulation set in motion three inevitable ecological consequences. First, as output from an ecosystem began to be increased, that system's ecological sustainability began to be reduced. As an example, in their book *Agricultural Ecology* (1979), Cox and Atkins show that as the agricultural manipulation of an ecosystem increases, and hence as nutrient off-take from that system increases, its inherent ecological sustainability is progressively impaired (chapter 11, p. 268). This can manifest itself in loss of soil structure, reduction in the amounts of soil nutrients available to vegetation, soil erosion, and a general disruption in the return of nutrients to the system via the detritus food-chains, and hence in the cycling of energy within the whole system.

Secondly, the increase in the output of resources from its habitat allowed this manipulative human population to increase to a level at which it needed to colonize new areas. The significance of this is that with the overflow population went the practice of the manipulation of the environment, which in turn facilitated further increases in the overflow population, necessitating yet further land colonization. In this way, the geographical spread of the human population and of the principle of environmental manipulation was set in motion.

Thirdly, through their emergent, manipulative involvement with their physical environment, I believe that the relationship between the human population and its environment began to change. Instead of simply being in a given region which had, up till then, provided a sufficiency of resources, the new *manipulators* as we might now call them, put so much knowing, conceptualized work into their habitat, that they began to develop a new type of affinity with it. Previously, grains had been gathered and consumed in the same year, but now they were stored as seed for next season, and planted in accessible, cleared patches, for ease of harvesting. Before, animals were hunted, but now they were driven into enclosed areas for ease of husbanding. Such a change was profound in that it required sustained human attention to the area in which the grain was planted, or in which the driven animals were enclosed. It required a much more discerning attitude towards the growth requirements of plants and animals – that is, towards their actual cultivation and husbandry – than had been necessary up till then.

And as the human work on a given environment intensified, the quality of the human relationship with, and attitude towards that environment gradually evolved. Where before the environment had supported and effectively 'looked after' a group of human beings, the result had been that a *sense of belonging* had prevailed. Now, however, since the human beings had begun to husband and 'look after' the environment, the feeling began to develop, I believe, that a specific environment could actually *belong to* the group of human beings who were tending it and doing all the work upon it.

Something along these lines must have occurred, I believe. 'After all', a conceptualizing manipulator of that time might have thought to him/herself, 'haven't I put all this effort and attention into this land to make it as productive as it now is? And since I have taken on the responsibility of its upkeep and maintenance, I have a greater claim to it than anybody else. If it belongs to anybody, it belongs to me!'

Even though such a development in lifestyle and attitude might have taken thousands of years to evolve, once it had taken hold, the work input of subsequent generations of either the same family or the same human community could have only served to reinforce the feeling that a given habitat actually *belonged to* that family or human community. Thus, by the time the twentieth generation of a family was contributing its efforts to enhancing the output from a given piece of land, the people involved would have had a *profound* feeling that that area of land really did *belong to* them. In this way, I believe, the concept of ownership began to take root.

However, this conceptual development subsequently involved the acceptance of a notion which has absolutely no meaningful ecological basis whatsoever. It required the attempting conceptualizers to accept the idea that the resources they now felt they *owned* were completely unavailable to, and hence absolutely *separated from*, all the other members of their community or group. Conversely, an acceptance of the concept of ownership required the other members of the community to acknowledge that they themselves were precluded from using the now 'owned' resources, and that they were consequently separated from those resources.

Yet such notions have no meaningful ecological basis because, as we established earlier, humankind is part of an absolutely cohesive ecological existence. In ecological reality, no component of this Earth, or indeed of this Universe, is *separable* from any other part or component. Therefore, the idea that a given resource or, for example, a portion of land could be a part of the lives of the 'owners' of that resource, but that thereby the same resource was *separated from* the lives and existence of everybody else, was, quite simply, without any ecological foundation.

Nonetheless, this concept of separability apparently did take hold, and must have been accepted as the premise upon which the concept of ownership was to be built up.

We can now consider the first of our two possibilities, the community which did *not* manipulate and ecologically exploit its environment, but lived *within* the natural yield-capacity of its region. This group would have included nomadic tribes as well as more regionally based communities. Their numbers remained low, their so-called standard of material living remained, we would say, basic, but the pressure they exerted on their environment would have remained fully supportable, since that environment's ecological integrity was not being transgressed. Thus its resources were not exhausted, and its sustainability was not impaired.

This could have been the case, I believe, for either settled or nomadic communities, since nomadism is merely one of the techniques which, although applied to an extended region, assists indigenous peoples in ensuring that the unmanipulated, ecological rates of resource-supply of a region are not transgressed.

Such human groups we might reasonably call *harmonizers*, and some have exemplified the sustainability of their ecological lifestyle by having thrived right up to the present day. The Panare of Venezuela, the Eskimos of Alaska and the Arctic, the Pygmies of the Central African rain forests, the Indians of North America and the Aborigines of Australia immediately spring to mind as groups of human beings who have only recently, in ecological terms, been affected by the predations of their more manipulative brothers and sisters. Up until that time they had all managed to retain an ecologically harmonious lifestyle which had ensured their sustainability.

That there remain so few is not because their lifestyles, being primitive, have been insufficient to ensure their long-term survival; they have survived. Rather, their depleted numbers bear testimony to the fact that as soon as other communities in the human family espoused more conceptualized, manipulative and exploitative lifestyles, such ecologically harmonious groups immediately became *exploitable*. And exploited they have been, in spite of the fact that their lifestyles are a distillation of intuitive, ecological sensitivity and sensibility, which has evolved since the commencement of human evolution upon this Earth.

We can perhaps hypothesize about the nature of the approach 'manipulators' might have employed, as they came across 'harmonizers' whose land and resources they wanted to colonize. In so doing, I think we might be able to see how these manipulators, who had begun to feel that habitats and resources *belonged to* them, had in fact *distanced* themselves from the very resources they wanted to possess. The following is a distillation of conversations that must have occurred over millenia as a 'manipulator-owner' confronted a 'harmonizer' whose land he/she wanted:

Manipulator: Hello, there. The land you inhabit is very beautiful. I wonder whether you realize that because you live in this place, and because you take so much care of this area, it really, sort of belongs to you; like your arm belongs to your body, you sort of own this land, you know.

Harmonizer: Oh well, I never thought of it like that. We all just use what is to hand, and we're very grateful for all that is available to us. And I must say, I really don't understand what you're saying. You see we all feel that we are part of our habitat. So if I am part of my habitat, and you say, I 'own' my habitat, then that means I also 'own' myself. What do I need to do that for? I already *am* myself.

Manipulator: Ah well, you learn something every day, don't you? In fact I really do think this land is beautiful and would like to use bits of it. However, since you own the area, I wouldn't dream of doing so without giving you something for the privilege. Here, have these fruits, nuts and implements.

Harmonizer: Well really, that's very kind of you, but you've no need to bother, you are always welcome to use as much land as you need.

Manipulator: No, I insist. You have these things that I have brought for you, and in return you can let me own some bits of your land, so that I can live on it and use it.

Harmonizer: Well thank you very much. And if you are short of anything just let me know.

Manipulator: Thank you.

As I appreciate, this hypothesized conversation is simplistic and brief, but in essence I believe this is the sort of dialogue which occurred and which allowed ownership-oriented people to infuse other people with the same notion. For many indigenous peoples, such an initiation proved to be the thin end of a wedge that ultimately led to the complete expropriation of their lands and resources.

The proud tribe of the Nez Perce (Pierced Nose) Indians was led by a most remarkable man named Hin-mah-too-yah-lat-kekht – Thunder Travelling to Loftier Mountain Heights – or Chief Joseph. His affection for the land out of which he came never ceased, and Chief Joseph was unremitting in his attempts to remain in the valleys and mountains of his birthplace. In this passage he makes clear (as he was always accustomed to do) his sentiments regarding ownership of the earth.

'The earth was created by the assistance of the sun, and it should be left as it was... The country was made without lines of demarcation, and it is no man's business to divide it... I see the whites all over the country gaining wealth, and see their desire to give us lands which are worthless... The earth and myself are of one mind. The measure of the land and the measure of our bodies are the same. Say to us if you can say it, that you were sent by the Creative Power to talk to us. Perhaps you think the Creator sent you here to dispose of us as you see fit. If I thought you were sent by the Creator I might be induced to think you had a right to dispose of me. Do not misunderstand me, but understand me fully with reference to my affection for the land, I never said the land was mine to do with it as I chose. The one who has the right to dispose of it is the one who created it. I claim a right to live on my land, and accord you the privilege to live on yours.'

A chief of one of the principal bands of the northern Blackfeet, upon being asked by U. S. delegates for his signature to one of the first land treaties in his region of the Milk River, near the northern border of Montana and the Northwest Territories, responds with a rejection of the money values of the white man.

'Our land is more valuable than your money. It will last forever. It will not even perish by the flames of fire. As long as the sun shines and the waters flow, this land will be here to give life to men and animals. We cannot sell the lives of men and animals; therefore we cannot sell this land. It was put here for us by the Great Spirit and we cannot sell it because it does not belong to us. You can count your money and burn it within the nod of a buffalo's head, but only the Great Spirit can count the grains of sand and the blades of grass of these plains. As a present to you, we will give you anything we have that you can take with you; but the land, never.'

(From Touch the Earth, 1971, ed. T. C. McLuhan)

Looking at the previous conversation more closely, in effect, what the manipulators were saying to the indigenous people was:

(a) We acknowledge that as things stand at the moment, the land and resources you use are *not available to us* for our own use.

(b) To use a label, you 'own' the land and resources yourselves.

(c) We wish to use some of your land and resources ourselves, so therefore we will give you something for it. Then we will own some of it and we can use it for our own purposes.

It is the first of those three statements which is the critical one. This is the part of the thought process in which the manipulators show that in order to obtain resources which they could subsequently manipulate, and which they could thereby feel they owned, they first had to accept that such resources were *permanently unavailable* to them. They had to conceive of the notion that any lands or resources currently in use by say, indigenous people, were *inaccessible* to them and were *permanently separated* from them for the purposes of their own utilization.

Now such a notion differs profoundly from that enshrined in the ancient practice of usufruct, in which people acknowledge that resources being used by other people are unavailable to them whilst they are thus being used; but that thereafter, the resources become freely available again for anybody else to use. (See, for example, Murray Bookchin's chapter on 'The outlook of organic society', in his book *The Ecology of Freedom*, 1982, p. 50.) In the practice of usufruct, resources are not *permanently* unavailable to all but the user; only temporarily, during their actual use.

However, the 'manipulators' had to conceive of the notion that resources could be *permanently* separated from them; that they could be permanently precluded from using them. This must have been the case; why else would they have made the effort to give 'fruits, nuts and implements' in exchange for the use of certain resources? What else would have necessitated the conceptualization of a new practice of 'owning' resources? All such people had to do, according to the old practice of usufruct, was either to use other freely available resources, or simply to wait.

But rather than do this, the would-be owners chose to accept the premise that a resource could be completely and permanently *separated* from them and completely and permanently unavailable to them and that by then paying something for it, the use of that resource could come completely and permanently to them, via 'ownership'. From an ecological point of view, the acceptance of this premise is utterly and absolutely without foundation or meaning. In ecological reality, nothing can be 'completely and permanently separated' from anything else.

In the ultimate analysis, all human beings are *part of* the Earth's store of resources and energy. Ultimately, we become those resources and the resources become us in the cycling of our global ecosystem. Over ecological time, nothing is separated from us nor can it be unavailable to us. Therefore, we don't need ownership; we don't need to 'own' resources to make them available for our use; we are part of them.

The ecologically meaningless assumption of separability that is enshrined in the concept of ownership persists right up to the present day. Thus, intrinsic in the effort any of us might make today to obtain a given article, say by working and saving up money for it, so that we can eventually bring it into our ownership, is the accepted premise that before purchase, the article, the product or the resource in question is not available for our use; that it is dislocated or separated from us. But in ecological reality this can never be the case because, as claimed throughout this work, every resource, every ecological entity, every atom and every component in our global ecosystem coheres with, and is part of, all other ecological entities and components.

In an ecologically cohesive reality, the concept of ownership is not valid, because it presupposes an ecological impossibility: namely separability.

***

In this, our initial consideration of ownership, I have referred to the *premise* which must be applied if the notion of ownership is to have any meaning, and have attempted to indicate that this premise embodies an ecological impossibility or unreality; namely the separation of one thing from another.

The example of the manipulator and the harmonizer illustrates that the notion of separability is needed *before* the concept of ownership can be seen to have any meaning at all; that is, it is needed as a premise for the conceptualization of ownership. However, if we consider a second example, we can see that the concept of ownership also requires acceptance of the notion of separability *after* it has been put into effect.

Let us briefly consider the ownership of land once again. Where a piece of land is bought and taken into ownership, then that piece of land is made available for its new owner's utilization. He or she can feel concern about what happens to that piece of land and can decide in what way it is used. However, *other* pieces of land in the region owned by others are *not* available for his or her utilization, and the way these other pieces of land are used is of no concern to him or her.

This means that wherever the notion of ownership is applied, in terms of concern for, responsibility for and utilization of that resource, those sections which are *not* in your ownership are *separated from* you. The result is that your ownership of one portion of a resource-system – say several acres of land in a given region – *enforces* a subsequent *dislocation of concern* from all the other portions of land in that region which you do *not* own.

In a recent *Guardian* article (17 February 1989) a good example of this phenomenon was presented, but on an international scale, rather than at a regional level:

Landowners Claim Rights on Amazon (by Jan Rocha in Sao Paulo)

The murdered Amazon leader, Chico Mendes, is being revered as an ecological martyr around the world, but in Brazil the international repercussions of his death have aroused a right-wing reaction with the slogan 'The Amazon is ours'.

'The Amazon is ours to do what we like with. We have the right to clear it and grow food to feed Brazilians,' said

Mr. Ronaldo Caiado, the president of the right wing land-owners'organization, the Rural Democratic Union (UDR).

He accused the English and the Americans of ecological imperialism and the Brazilian left wing of being their lackeys.

This illustrates the point that if the English and the American protagonists *themselves* acknowledge the rights conferred by the ownership of resources in their own countries, then they cannot easily dismiss Mr Caiado's point of view, even if his attitude *is* contributing to the rapid destruction of the Brazilian rain forest. According to those rights, the Brazilian Amazon belongs to the Brazilian landowners, and is theirs to do with as they wish. On the basis of ownership, the Amazon is no concern of the English, nor of the Americans.

To summarize this section on ownership, we can therefore say that the concept of ownership requires the acceptance of a *separation* from our resource-base, both before its implementation, that is as a premise, and after its implementation, that is as a consequence. However, in an ecologically *cohesive* reality such a requirement cannot be met, and therefore we can reasonably conclude that there is no ecologically meaningful basis for the concept of ownership.

***

If we now look at the current global situation in terms of ownership, we will, I believe, discover a truly amazing fact. Not only have the conceptualization and the institutionalization of ownership spread right round our globe, but also the resources that have thereby been 'owned', are now concentrated in the hands of a relatively small minority of people. Consequently, the majority of humankind is now *indeed* separated, at least institutionally, from its resource-base.

Data on resource-ownership in general, and on the skewed distribution of ownership in particular, is amazingly scant, especially in view of its fundamental global importance. This is the case in developing and developed countries alike, and for me, the very paucity of the data speaks volumes.

Richard Norton-Taylor, in his invaluable book *Whose Land is it Anyway?* (1982), has in fact courageously faced up to this situation and has compiled an overview of the situation in Britain:

> The distribution of income has been the subject of a great deal of controversy over recent years. But the absence of a debate over the ownership of land and property is remarkable, given the concentration of landed wealth in so few hands and that it is such a visible source of wealth, including unearned wealth. 'Throughout the period we can collectively remember,' noted A. H. Halsey, Oxford University professor of social and administrative studies, in his 1978 Reith Lectures, 'three-quarters of us have been virtually property-less in that area which covers the central part of our lives and our occupations – how we earn a living and how we relate ourselves to our fellow men... A tiny minority has monopolised wealth, and an even tinier minority has monopolised property for power.'
>
> He was describing all kinds of property but the inequalities of land ownership are even more striking. Just over 1 per cent of the adult population owns almost seventy per cent of the land [Royal Commission on the Distribution of Income and Wealth, report no. 7, 1979]. The concentration of land ownership in Britain, encouraged by the Enclosures and Industrial Revolution, is unique in Europe. Elsewhere, political and social revolutions led to a more drastic break-up of large estates. On the Continent, the aristocracy and traditional landed classes failed to hold on to their interests; in Britain, they have a subtler instinct, they knew how to compromise politically. And in Britain the aristocracy was shielded from the Napoleonic Code whereby property is divided among the family; primogeniture continued in Britain where property was handed down to the eldest son.
>
> Inheritance therefore played a much more significant part in the pattern of land ownership in Britain than in other countries. It still does so: the relative decline in ownership of wealth enjoyed by the top 1 per cent has been picked up by the group (the 2 – 5 per cent of the most wealthy) immediately below the very top [A. B. Atkinson and A. J. Harrison, *Distribution of Personal Wealth in Britain*, Cambridge University Press, 1978)]. Because the bulk of the property is distributed among the family before the death of the owner often so as to

avoid taxes, the wealth of rich families has been distributed among rich families.

Seventy-five per cent of the total personal wealth of the richest 1 per cent is transmitted, inherited, wealth. This accounts for more than half of the wealth of the top five per cent. The bottom 50 per cent in the wealth table own less than 1 per cent of all land.

The Ownership of Land (in the UK)

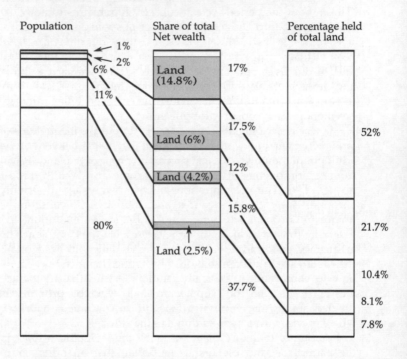

The concentration of wealth is even more significant when it comes to farm land ownership. Britain's farmland is owned by just 2 per cent of the population. The trend towards fewer and fewer farms continues: 10 per cent of all farms – the biggest – produce half of all the food grown in Britain. Half the food grown in Britain .comes from land owned by 0.2 per cent of the population.

'Knowledge of ownership is a matter of hearsay and local gossip, rather than any statutory and central register of landownership. A lovely anachronism of England. Long may it remain' – Peter Wormell, farmer of 900 acres in Essex, former member of Essex County Council, the Water Board and his local rural district council.

'The paucity of comprehensive up-to-date information on landownership is remarkable' – 7th report of the Royal Commission on the Distribution of Income and Wealth.

(From *Whose Land Is It Anyway?*, 1982, by Richard Norton-Taylor)

Whilst information on ownership is thin on the ground in the United Kingdom, it is virtually non-existent in the developing countries of the world. Nonetheless, an indication of the ownership situation worldwide has recently been presented in *New Internationalist* magazine (*see overleaf*).

As a result of the observation of this current global situation we can say that the effective 'separation' of humankind from its resource-base has actually been implemented on a world-wide basis, and throughout much of human society. Resources are *not* now freely available to the vast majority of humankind. They have been 'owned away' from them. The bulk of humankind has been dislocated from immediate access to its resource-base, of which it is ecologically a part, by the institutionalization of the concept of ownership. Ownership, rather than being a means of acquisition, has shown itself to be a tool of deprivation.

In this way, the global institutionalization of the concept of ownership has created the premise it needed in the first place, but didn't have. It has created the effective separation of the majority of humankind from its resource-base, and this very separation now furnishes the drive for ownership. Thus, paradoxically, humankind can currently only gain access to its resource-base via ownership, when in fact ownership has been the means of its inital dispossesion.

In essence, ownership requires separation as a premise, creates effective separation, and by so doing creates a perpetual requirement for itself. Sounds a bit like conceptualization, doesn't it?

LAND IN WHOSE HANDS? – THE FACTS

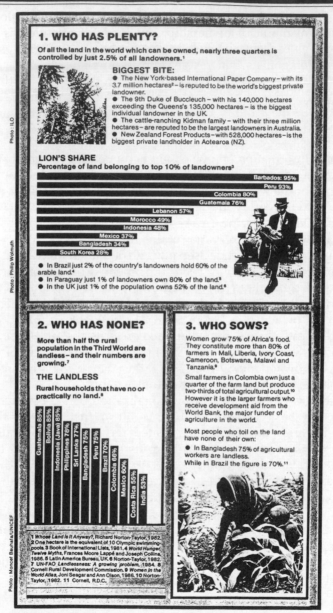

1. WHO HAS PLENTY?

Of all the land in the world which can be owned, nearly three quarters is controlled by just 2.5% of all landowners.[1]

BIGGEST BITE:
● The New York-based International Paper Company – with its 3.7 million hectares[2] – is reputed to be the world's biggest private landowner.
● The 9th Duke of Buccleuch – with his 140,000 hectares exceeding the Queen's 135,000 hectares – is the biggest individual landowner in the UK.
● The cattle-ranching Kidman family – with their three million hectares – are reputed to be the largest landowners in Australia.
● New Zealand Forest Products – with 528,000 hectares – is the biggest private landholder in Aotearoa (NZ).

Photo : ILO

LION'S SHARE
Percentage of land belonging to top 10% of landowners[3]

Barbados: 95%
Peru 93%
Colombia 80%
Guatemala 76%
Lebanon 57%
Morocco 49%
Indonesia 48%
Mexico 37%
Bangladesh 34%
South Korea 28%

● In Brazil just 2% of the country's landowners hold 60% of the arable land.[4]
● In Paraguay just 1% of landowners own 80% of the land.[5]
● In the UK just 1% of the population owns 52% of the land.[6]

Photo : Philip Wolmuth

2. WHO HAS NONE?

More than half the rural population in the Third World are landless – and their numbers are growing.[7]

THE LANDLESS
Rural households that have no or practically no land.[8]

Guatemala 85%
Bolivia 85%
Indonesia (Java) 85%
Philippines 78%
Sri Lanka 77%
Bangladesh 75%
Peru 75%
Brazil 70%
Colombia 66%
Mexico 60%
Costa Rica 55%
India 53%

Photo : Maciel Bauhain/UNICEF

3. WHO SOWS?

Women grow 75% of Africa's food. They constitute more than 80% of farmers in Mali, Liberia, Ivory Coast, Cameroon, Botswana, Malawi and Tanzania.[9]

Small farmers in Colombia own just a quarter of the farm land but produce two-thirds of total agricultural output.[10] However it is the larger farmers who receive development aid from the World Bank, the major funder of agriculture in the world.

Most people who toil on the land have none of their own:
● In Bangladesh 75% of agricultural workers are landless. While in Brazil the figure is 70%.[11]

1 *Whose Land is it Anyway?*, Richard Norton-Taylor, 1982.
2 One hectare is the equivalent of 10 Olympic swimming-pools. 3 Book of International Lists, 1981. 4 *World Hunger, Twelve Myths*, Frances Moore Lappé and Joseph Collins, 1986. 5 Latin America Bureau, UK. 6 Norton-Taylor, 1982. 7 UN-FAO *Landlessness: A growing problem*, 1984. 8 Cornell Rural Development Commission. 9 *Women in the World Atlas*, Joni Seagar and Ann Olson, 1986. 10 Norton-Taylor, 1982. 11 Cornell, R.D.C.

At this juncture I should like to make what I consider to be an extremely important qualification. In undertaking an ecological evaluation of the concept of ownership and the subsequent global institutionalization of ownership, my focus of attention is on *ownership* as concept and institution, not on the two groups of human protagonists that result from its implementation – the 'resource-owners' and the 'resourceless'. In my view *both* these parties are wronged by ownership. The owner is deluded into believing in the validity of his/her privilege, whilst the non-owner is deceived into accepting his/her dislocation from the Earth's resource-base. Both positions are profoundly deluded and distorted. The *concept of ownership itself*, I believe, is where the focus of attention must lie.

'Never mind the imbalance look at the pivot'

Therefore this ecological evaluation of ownership is not intended solely for land-owners and resource-controllers who own and control a disproportionate share of land and resources, and who honestly believe that such ownership and control are the only means of 'managing' such resources successfully. Nor is it aimed at the millions of people who own tiny parcels of global resources, e.g. home-owners, people who own a garden plot or small workshop, and who feel that such ownership is a critically important means of defending the tiny quantity of resources that *are* available to them. Nor is it intended just for those millions of people round the globe who own, as near as damn it, absolutely no resources whatsoever. It is intended for *all* people, in the hope that we can *all* put the concept and institution of ownership into an ecological perspective and see that it is injuring *all* of us in its insistence on an effective separation from our resource-base.

Living on 'enough' is really disarming

As I have said, at some point in our ecologically recent past, groups of human beings began to attempt to conceptualize. Subsequently, such groups sought to manipulate their immediate environments in order to extract more resources from those environments than would have been naturally forthcoming. That is, they began to transgress, or break through, their habitats' inherent ecological parameters and their habitats' inherent, ecological rates of resource-supply. They wanted to obtain more than the *resource-sufficiency* which their habitat had provided up to that point, and which had facilitated their evolution till then. This, I believe, was the first-ever act of physical, ecological aggression, perpetrated by a newly conceptualizing humankind. It took the form of conceptualized, physical aggression against the ecological parameters and capacities inherent in the immediate habitat. It was, shall we say, 'human:habitat' aggression.

The increases in the human population that ensued resulted in the colonizing of new habitats and the spread of human:habitat aggression. However, it is extremely important for us to appreciate that *all other* groups of human beings existing elsewhere at that time in an ecologically non-manipulative, harmonious way were, in fact, *part of* the greater environment which these now ecologically exploitative human groups were starting to colonize. Therefore, sooner or later it was inevitable that these ecologically exploitative groups would confront eco-logically-harmonious groups, and it was only at *this* juncture, I believe, that what we might call 'human:human' aggression occurred.

This implies that human:habitat aggression *preceded* human:human aggression; one inevitably leading to the other. Both human:habitat and human:human forms of conflict were instigated by ecologically aggressive groups, in their attempts to take and consume more resources from their habitat than the ecological sufficiency which would otherwise have ensured their physical survival and psychological well-being. And this threshold of ecological *resource-sufficiency* is, I believe, the line about which all aggressive and defensive activity, and hence about which all conflict, ebbs and flows.

The first aggressive stone and the first defensive stone were *both* taken up as different responses to the same pivotal point: whether or not to be *satisfied* with a sufficiency of essential resources.

In ecological reality therefore the very first form of conflict ever experienced by humankind occurred when our *newly conceptualized efforts to seek more* required us to break through *our intuitive ability to be satisfied with enough.*

To summarize our deliberations on the concept of conflict, therefore, we can make the following statements:

- the initial and most fundamental form of conflict experien-ced by humankind was that between the supposedly conceptual and the inherently intuitive; this form of conflict began to be experienced about the time at which efforts were undertaken to secure *more* resources from an environment than were intuitively felt to be *sufficient*.
- this initial form of conceptual versus intuitive conflict led human beings to break through, and hence come into

67

conflict with, the ecological integrities and natural limitations of their immediate habitat; in this way, human:habitat conflict arose.
- subsequently, as human:habitat conflict spread outwards to newly colonized areas, human:human conflict inevitably arose since, quite simply, all human beings other than the ecologically exploitative were part of the extended habitat which now stood to be colonized.

The *More* Ethic and Greed

Once the concept of ownership had spread to the new areas colonized by ecologically manipulative groups of human beings, the scene was set for the evolution of all the other concepts that today form the basis of our economic way of life. And the concept which might well have evolved close on the heels of ownership was that which we can call the '*more* ethic', or simply 'greed'.

In the world which preceded that in which ownership was established, there was, it would appear, an *evenness* in the distribution of resources amongst human beings. Murray Bookchin refers to this phenomenon in his book *The Ecology of Freedom* (1982, p. 144) and asserts that at that time there was a general recognition of what he calls 'the equality of unequals'. This is a recognition of the basic fact that every human being has to be able to obtain the resources he or she needs to survive physically and to achieve a general state of well-being, and that people differ in their ability to do this. This overall recognition was the result of a number of practices which are identified by Murray Bookchin. Firstly, and as already described, the practice of usufruct was prevalent. This is 'The freedom of individuals in a community to appropriate resources, merely by virtue of the fact that they are using them' (ibid., p. 50). Thus resources were available to human beings to the extent that they used them; and they used them to the extent that they needed them. This resulted in resources being distributed according to personal, ecological *need*.

Secondly there existed the practice of 'complementarity'; that is, 'the disinterested willingness to pool needed things and needed services'. This again contributed to an overall *evenness* in the distribution of resources and was itself based on a recognition of the fact that every human being has a basic minimum requirement for resources – the 'irreducible minimum' as Murray Bookchin calls it (ibid., pp. 143/4).

Together, these practices created a *compensatory* system which recognised that since each human being had a different ability to acquire the basic minimal resources needed to survive, the less able members of that community could count on the more able to make up any shortfall they might experience. Consequently, every individual received what she or he needed, to the extent that the habitat could provide it, and – and this is an important point – everybody was intuitively *satisfied* with that sufficiency. We can see this today in animal communities; when all of the basic essential *needs* of any one animal have been satisfied, the animal is satisfied, and it will rest contentedly for a while.

However, as population density began to increase, as human settlement and agriculture developed, and as the concept of ownership began to establish itself, a strain was placed on the ability of a community to continue to distribute resources according to need. In any one locality some resources were *not* now readily available to everybody according to need; some resources were 'owned' by specific families or one or two human beings, and their availability was thereby made less immediate.

One can imagine a situation in which the 'owner' of a resource which was in particularly short supply might have begun to feel the power which ownership of this particular resource conferred on him or her. Such an owner might have said to himself/herself: 'This salt-deposit which I own and work is of great importance to everybody in the community. People ought to be grateful to me for providing them with their salt, and if they are not, I might choose not to let them have any even if they really need it.'

In a later section, we will go on to consider how this situation led to the notion of the 'unbalanced exchange' of resources, but for now, the point I want to emphasize is that gradually people must have begun to perceive the *power* which was latent in the 'ownership' of vital resources. This power somehow magnified or inflated an owner's stature in his or her relationships with other members of the community. It made available to them a potential for dictating to their fellows in a way that was previously unknown, because through ownership they could threaten to *withhold* essential resources from the rest of the community if they so wished.

My reason for wanting to focus attention on the *power* which the ownership of resources began to confer is that once this power is perceived, it provides the rationale whereby human beings make the effort to take *more* resources into ownership. 'If the ownership of these vital resources gives me power over the other people in my community, then the ownership of *more* vital resources will give me *more* power.' That is, the new 'owner' of resources began to feel *dissatisfied*.

Up to this point in its evolution, I believe that humankind had intuitively felt that a 'sufficiency' was enough, and had been intuitively capable of being *satisfied* with just that. Now, however, the concept of ownership and the conceptualization of 'owning more' heralded a new possibility – the concept of dissatisfaction and hence of *greed*.

Thus it was not until the concept of owning or *having* resources had established itself, that the concept of *having more* could have evolved; that is, the conceptualization of ownership *preceded* the conceptualization of greed. This assertion is important in two respects: firstly, I am saying that the concept of 'greed', i.e. of 'having more', only became possible *after* the concept of ownership, i.e. of 'having', had evolved; secondly, I am saying that 'greed' is not inherent in real, human ecological 'being'.

Before the era in which it started its attempt to conceptualize, humankind existed in a completely un-self-realized manner. In an unconceptualized state of 'being', you can't 'be more' than you are being. Thus it was only *after* humankind started to attempt to conceptualize, followed by its attempt to conceptualize the ownership of resources and of *having* things, that the concept of *more* itself became a possibility. And 'having more' is the essence of greed.

As a final observation on the topic of the *more* ethic and greed, we can note that in ecological reality it is not possible to *continue* to be greedy. The excessive 'take' you enjoy now travels round the ecosystem you are exploiting as an extra 'give' by that ecosystem. As a consequence, the ecosystem gradually becomes depleted and, ultimately, it will only be able to furnish you with *less* than the sustainable ecological sufficiency it was offering you in the first place.

Ownership Necessitates *Exchange*

In the world which preceded that in which the ownership of resources was established there was a free-flow of resources from a community's habitat to its members, according to *need*. Since the requirements of individual human beings varied, and since their abilities to procure what they required also varied, in general the fitter members of a community would contribute more to the community than they took from it, so that the extra needs of the less able members could be satisfied.

This is, I believe, a reasonable summary of the notion already mentioned and referred to by Murray Bookchin in his book *The Ecology of Freedom* as the 'equality of unequals'; and if we look at the theory behind the 'equality of unequals', we discover how important the system was in ensuring the survival of as many human beings as possible in any given community.

Whilst it is true that all individuals, in absolute terms, have different requirements, psychological and physical, for ensuring their survival, in percentage terms each one of us has to obtain 100 per cent of our actual *needs*, to survive. Therefore in percentage terms there is an evenness in our real needs, because we *all* need to get 100 per cent of them. Diagramatically, we can show this as in Figure 1 overleaf.

Still thinking in percentage terms, the relative capability of each individual to achieve the 100 per cent of his or her own resource needs, however, varies widely; some individuals are capable of providing, shall we say, 110 per cent of their

71

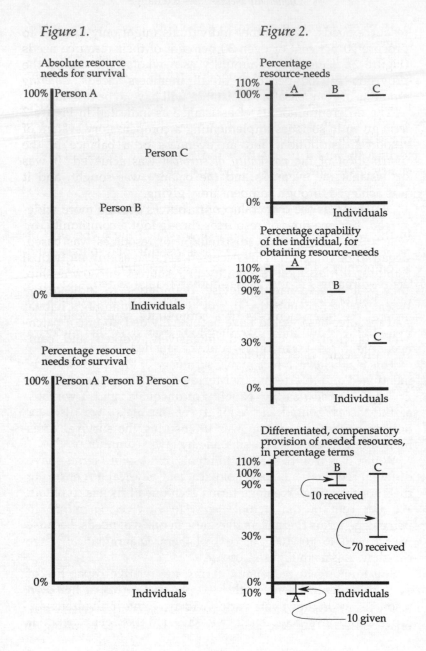

Figure 1.

Figure 2.

resource needs, whilst other individuals might only manage to procure 90 per cent or even 30 per cent of their resource needs (Figure 2). Thus, if a community as a whole is to ensure the provision of 100 per cent of all members' needs, *differing* amounts of compensatory assistance will have to be provided.

The different amounts of assistance as indicated in Figure 2 *were* given in societies implementing a compensatory system of resource distribution, and an evenness or a balance in the distribution of the *possibility of survival* was achieved. It was in *this* that the evenness and the balance was sought, and it was achieved through compensatory giving.

However, as the ownership of resources became more wide-spread, the free-flow of resources throughout a community, on which this compensatory distribution of resources was based, began to be impeded. This occurred because as any individual family or group took a quantity of resources into ownership, they would have had to devise 'boundaries' to indicate the extent of their ownership. In this way, a community's habitat and resource-base would have become divided up into a patch-work of clearly demarcated, intensively worked and com-munally acknowledged holdings.

Ownership boundaries, and hence ownership barriers, now criss-crossed a hitherto undemarcated landscape, resulting in the need to devise a facility which allowed the movement of 'owned' resources across these ownership barriers. It was the *exchange of resources* that provided this new facility.

In this way the development of ownership eventually required the *exchange* of owned resources; and the first form of exchange would, I believe, have been a *balanced* exchange of resources.

A Balanced Exchange of Resources Necessitates an Effective Separation from Concern for Other People's Survival

Where a human being or a group of human beings 'own' a resource, they can monitor and control the use of that resource. They have jurisdiction over the giving and withholding of that resource and this allows them to trim and regulate the amount of that resource which flows outwards to others in the community.

'I'll give you six bags of wheat, if you give me a goat and three hens. That'll be fair, I think, don't you?'

In early barter or exchange systems this capacity to regulate and control the flow of owned resources made it possible for 'reasonable' or 'fair' swaps of resources to be negotiated.

Thus I believe the early exchanges of resources involved the exchange of *balanced* amounts of resource, and on the face of it, this would certainly seem to have been 'fair enough'. But on further consideration I think we shall find that this is not, in fact, the case. As more and more resources were taken into ownership, it was inevitable that certain individuals and human groups ended up with small amounts of resources, whilst others ended up owning large amounts of resources. The consequence of this was that those with little had few resources to exchange, whilst those with lots had large amounts of resources to exchange. Thus, 'exchange-power' developed in proportion to the extent of your resource-holdings; you could enter into the exchange of resources only to the extent that you already owned resources (see p. 77). And herein lies a paradox: those human beings with few resources were the very ones who, *for the purpose of ensuring their survival*, needed to receive relatively *more* resources than those with large resource-holdings. To use the terminology we employed earlier, they needed to receive *compensatory* amounts of resources to make good any shortfall they may have been suffering. But where the *balanced* exchange of resources had become the only mode of resource interaction between members of a community, such compensatory giving was no longer possible. In a balanced exchange of resources you only receive according to what you can give in exchange – *you get according to what you already have, not according to what you need.*

Therefore, whilst on the surface the concept of a balanced exchange of resources seems fair and equitable in terms of the exchange itself; in terms of ensuring that people get what they need to survive, it is not. And it is not fair and equitable in terms of ensuring that people get what they need to survive because it does not *compensate* individuals for any shortfalls they may have in owned resources, nor for any variations that might exist in their individual needs.

We are therefore driven to conclude that the very notion of a balanced exchange of resources is founded upon an acceptance of a dislocation or separation from any real concern for ensuring the survival of other members of a human community. This differs profoundly from the compensatory system of resource distribution which existed before, and which, as we said, was based upon a free-flow of resources throughout a community, according to need. This system had evolved in an attempt to ensure that *all* the members of a community survived, to the extent that the habitat could provide.

What is more, as resource-ownership continued to spread, the exchange of resources, as opposed to the compensatory-giving of resources, increased, which in turn must have increased the insistence by resource-owners that *balanced* exchanges of resources be achieved. That is, over perhaps thousands of years:

'balancing the amounts of resources exchanged'

stood to become more important than

'balancing the chances of survival '.

As a child, I understood how to give. I have forgotten this grace, since I became civilised.

From a speech by Ohiyesa,
a Santee Dakota Indian (1858 – 1939).
(*Touch the Earth*, 1971, ed. T. C. McLuhan)

The ground was thus prepared for a situation in which it was more important to ensure that the exchange of resources was in balance than to ensure that a fellow human being should survive. A development along these lines is what must have occurred, because this situation is precisely the one we have today. International authorities such as the IMF, OECD, EEC, the World Bank, GATT, etc. now preside over our worldwide systems of exchange, and ensure that these systems balance, in spite of being aware that people in various parts of the world are dying because they have no access to, nor the means of acquiring, absolutely essential resources for survival.

Today's most blatant example of this is to be witnessed in the discrepancy in resource-availability between the developed 'North' and the developing 'South'. In the 1980s, the industrialized North has resource surpluses, whilst the 'under-developed' South is resource-poor. How can the industrialized North not *give* its surpluses to satisfy the real needs of the resource-poor South? The answer is that it would wreck the *balance sheets* of the international *exchange* system: the destitute South does not have sufficient resources with which to join in on the merry game of exchange. Balance has to be achieved in terms of the *exchange mechanism*, even though millions of human beings are dying as a direct result.

In seeking to achieve balanced exchanges of resources, it would appear that human individuals had to effectively dislocate themselves, or separate themselves from their customary, indeed evolutionary concern for ensuring the survival of other members of the human family.

The Development from Balanced to Unbalanced Exchanges of Resources

As I said earlier, the extent to which any human individual or group of human beings can become involved in exchange dealings is underpinned by the quantity of resources held in ownership. This draws our attention to a consideration of how different amounts and values of resource-holdings came to be owned by different people. How did some people acquire valuable

77

resources, whilst other got only a few or no resources at all? This is a significant question because it was these initial differentials in resource-holdings that gave various members of a community different amounts of exchange-power. In turn, it was the perception of differing amounts of exchange-power, I believe, that caused some members of communities to indulge in *unbalanced* rather than balanced exchanges of resources. Let us therefore consider how such differentials in resource-holding might have arisen.

The spread of the process whereby resources were taken into ownership was, I believe, an *ad hoc* process which took perhaps tens of thousands of years to establish itself. Inevitably, the best items or areas of any resource would have been taken into ownership first, so that any late-comers would have ended up with less valuable holdings. In addition, and in view of the variability of the resource-base that was being brought into ownership, it is inevitable that at all stages throughout the process, the value of resources owned by human beings must have differed widely. It was these initial differentials in resource-holdings that furnished their owners with different amounts of resources, not only to consume, but also to exchange, and as a result, individual owners found themselves with differing degrees of exchange-power.

Thus, the owner of a lot of resources, or of highly valued resources, could become extensively engaged in resource-exchanges because of the exchange-power he wielded, whilst the owner of few resources could not. Significantly, therefore, the extent to which resource-owners could become involved in exchange dealings was no longer related to real *need*, but to the extent of their resource-holdings and hence to their exchange-power. What is more, the owner of a lot of resources knew that whatever happened in any exchange of resources, he or she would still have sufficient to ensure survival. But the owner of few resources – and even more so, the owner of fewer resources than were essential for survival – did *not* have this feeling of resource-security. For him or her the outcome of the exchange could literally mean the difference between life and death.

Gradually the resource-rich owners began to feel, I believe, that because the less well-off owners were in greater need, they were in a *weakened* bargaining position. The resource-rich owners knew that if the less well-off people didn't get the resources they needed, they might actually perish. Consequently, such resource-rich owners began to feel that their ownership of resources gave them an *enhanced exchange-power*, and that they could therefore *dictate* the conditions of exchange. Because of this enhanced exchange-power, and as the concept of greed took root, I believe that they began to exact *more* resources from their needy, not-so-well-off fellows, than they gave in return.

As we noted earlier, the evolution of the balanced exchanging of resources resulted in the focus of attention being concentrated on balancing the system of exchange, rather than on ensuring human survival. Here, however, with the development of the *unbalanced* exchanging of resources, we see the concentration on the exchange-mechanism going so far that not only is concern with human survival neglected, it is positively exploited.

Thus over perhaps thousands of years a transition took place from a system in which the resources exchanged were at least of roughly equal value in terms of their contribution to human survival, to a system in which the exchanges of resources were intentionally unfavourable to the less well off owner. That is, balanced exchanges of resources gave way to unbalanced exchanges.

From Him That Hath Not … Shall be Taken Away

At this point, I think it is important for us to note that the power these resource-rich owners felt they possessed was a very strange sort of power. It was a power which said that in any exchange of life-essential resources, a well-provisioned person could exact *more* resources from a less well-off person than he or she gave in return. As such, it was the very antithesis of what had happened in the *compensatory*, pre-ownership days, when, to the extent that resources were available, each person had received according to *need*, to ensure his or her survival.

Therefore, instead of the needy receiving whatever they required to survive, the development in awareness of this new exchange-power meant that they stood to lose even their insufficiency.

This development from a *compensatory* flow of resources to an *unbalanced exchange* really represented, I believe, a qualitative about-face, ushering in what we might call an inversion of real, ecological sensibility; that is, from the *nurturing* of human survival to its *exploitation*.

Previously need had engendered spontaneous help; now, it triggered 'greed' and exploitation.

Thus today, the international community is responding to the developing countries' lack of funds by *lending* them money at low interest rates, with the result that in 1988, for example, '... *they* gave *us* net aid of £43 billion in debt repayments.... the wealthier nations have now become parasites on the poor.' (Article by Brian Leith, *The Listener* 16 November, 1989: World Bank Statistics).

The obverse of this phenomenon is that resources are channelled to populations with exchange power, but with no real *need* for more resources. For example, in Europe a milk production stimulant is currently being developed for dairy cows at a time when milk over-production has necessitated the imposition of production quotas.

It is economically expedient and hence profitable for these situations to exist, irrespective of the fact that in terms of satisfying human *needs* they make no sense at all.

Realization of this fact caused a certain agricultural student, in the early 1980s, to comment: 'In today's modern agriculture, food is a by-product'.

To give another example, you might think that where the medical, scientific and technological knowledge existed, or could be developed, then vaccines would be produced that could save the lives of hundreds of thousands of Third World children from endemic diseases; but you would be wrong. In a *Guardian* article (11 March 1988) Tim Radford reported:

Vaccine costs 'Threaten Third World Children'

Millions of children in the developing world are at risk from killing or crippling diseases, because commercial firms are not prepared to invest in vaccines for them, two US scientists have warned.

The scale of the problem is outlined in a paper today by Dr Anthony Robbins, of Boston University, and Dr Phyllis Freeman of the University of Massachusetts at a WHO conference in Tailloires, France, on protecting the world's children. Drs. Robbins and Freeman argue that the Expanded Programme on Immunisation (EPI), which last year delivered 600 million doses, has demonstrated how cheap vaccines can be. The six current vaccines – all developed more than 10 years ago – can be used to immunize a child for about £2.70...

But the problems begin with the development of new or improved vaccines against Aids, hepatitis B, malaria, yellow fever, cholera, typhoid, Japanese encephalitis, and other diseases. There are 21 vaccines which matter to the developing world, all of which could be ready within 10 years, but fewer than half of them could be expected to have significant world markets. The two doctors warn that commercial firms are not developing production capacity for third world sales.

Functioning within their framework of economic rationales, all commercially active enterprises today reason that they *have to* ensure the profitability of all their production systems and product-lines, so that they can generate investment capital for future research and development. In so doing, they are arguing for the acceptability of profit-orientated, unbalanced exchanges of resoures which, in a wider, ecological context, make no sense at all.

Today's economic imperative, in which the notion of the unbalanced exchange of resources is enshrined, is the very antithesis of an intuitive ecological sensibility that would strive to optimize human survival. 'Economic sense' is not *real* sense, there is a sort of inversion or 'twist' introduced into what is otherwise a natural, ecological cycle of perception and intuitive response.

81

This: becomes this:

This phenomenon was recognized several thousand years ago, as is shown by this excerpt from the *Tao Te Ching*:

> It is the way of heaven to take from what has in excess, in order to make good what is deficient. The way of man is otherwise. It takes from those who are in want in order to offer this to those who already have more than enough. Who is there who can take what he himself has in excess and offer this to the empire? Only he who has the way.
>
> (From *Tao Te Ching* by Lao Tzu, p. 139, verse 184a)

Similarly, in the Christian tradition, we have the same phenomenon expressed in the 'Parable of the Talents'.

> For the kingdom of heaven is as a man travelling into a far country, who called his own servants, and delivered unto them his goods. And unto one he gave five talents, to another two, to another one; to every man according to his several ability; and straightway took his journey. Then he that had received the five talents went and traded with the same, and made them other five talents. And likewise he that had received two, he also gained other two. But he that had received one went and digged in the earth, and hid his lord's money.
>
> After a long time the lord of these servants cometh, and reckoneth with them. And so he that had received five talents came and brought other five talents, saying, Lord, thou deliveredst unto me five talents: behold, I have gained beside them five talents more. His lord said unto him, Well done, thou good and faithful servant: thou hast been faithful over a few things, I will make thee ruler over many things: enter thou into the joy of thy lord. He also that had received two talents came and said,

Lord, thou deliveredst unto me two talents; behold, I have gained two other talents beside them. His lord said unto him, Well done thou good and faithful servant, thou hast been faithful over a few things, I will make thee ruler over many things: enter thou into the joy of they lord.

Then he which had received the one talent came and said, Lord I knew thee that thou art an hard man, reaping where thou hast not sown, and gathering where thou has not strawed: And I was afraid, and went and hid thy talent in the earth: lo, there thou hast that is thine. His lord answered and said unto him, Thou wicked and slothful servant, thou knewest that I reap where I sowed not, and gather where I have not strawed: Thou oughtest therefore to have put my money to the exchangers, and then at my coming I should have received mine own with usury. Take therefore the talent from him, and give it unto him that hath ten talents. For unto everyone that hath shall be given, and he shall have abundance: but from him that hath not shall be taken away even that which he hath. And cast ye the unprofitable servant into outer darkness: there shall be weeping and gnashing of teeth.

When the son of man shall come in his glory, and all the holy angels with him, then shall he sit upon the throne of his glory. And before him shall be gathered all nations: and he shall separate them one from another, as a shepherd divideth his sheep from the goats: And he shall set the sheep on his right hand, but the goats on the left. Then shall the King say unto them on his right hand, Come ye blessed of my father, inherit the kingdom prepared for you from the foundation of the world:

For I was an hungred, and ye gave me meat: I was thirsty, and you gave me drink: I was a stranger, and ye took me in.

Naked, and ye clothed me: I was sick, and ye visited me: I was in prison, and ye came unto me.

Then shall the righteous answer him, saying, Lord, when saw we thee an hungred, and fed thee? or thirsty, and gave thee drink?

When saw we thee a stranger, and took thee in? or naked, and clothed thee?

Or when saw we thee sick, or in prison, and came unto thee?

And the King shall answer and say unto them, Verily I say unto you, Inasmuch as ye have done it unto one of the least of these my brethren, ye have done it unto me.

Then shall he say also unto them on the left hand, Depart from me, ye cursed, into everlasting fire, prepare for the devil and his angels:

For I was an hungred,and ye gave me no meat: I was thirsty, and ye gave me no drink:

I was a stranger, and ye took me not in: naked, and ye clothed me not: sick, and in prison, and ye visited me not.

Then shall they also answer him, saying, Lord, when saw we thee an hungred, or thirsty, or a stranger, or naked, or sick, or in prison, and did not minister unto thee?

Then shall he answer them, saying, Verily I say unto you, Inasmuch as ye did it not to one of the least of these, ye did it not to me. And these shall go away into everlasting punishment: but the righteous into life eternal.

(Gospel According to St. Matthew 25:14 – 46)

In biblical terms, we can summarize the progression we have just described by saying that in essence:

The 'compensatory' free-flow of resources	was	'To him that hath not shall be given.'
The 'balanced' exchange of resources	was	'To him that hath not shall not be given.'
The 'unbalanced' exchange of resources	was	'From him that hath not shall be taken away.'

***

Whereas previously the balanced exchange of resources had resulted in an effective stagnation in the distribution of resources – that is, resources flowed amongst the 'haves' but not to or between the 'have-nots' – the unbalanced exchange of resources

84

just discussed did at least re-instil some dynamism into the situation. Resources did indeed begin to flow once again, between the 'have-nots' and the 'haves' but this time it was according to the terms set by the 'haves', and *not* according to the needs of the 'have-nots'. Thus the net movement of resources was incessantly towards the 'already-haves', and the new dynamism, instead of nurturing a *balance* in resource-distribution and the chances of survival, was one which inevitably exacerbated an *imbalance* in these processes.

Moreover, instead of being an ecologically spontaneous dynamism, instigated by human, ecological need, it was an enforced dynamism, motivated by conceptualized greed. This new dynamism, therefore, resulted in a steady increase in the *degree of imbalance* in resource-distribution among members of the human family, and set the scene for the final development in the maturing process of the unbalanced exchange of resources, in which it evolved into an ethic.

The 'profit-motive' is a *doctrine* of imbalance. It is a doctrine which enshrines the ethic of the unbalanced exchange of resources. According to the profit-motive, a deal can *only* be entered into if it brings about an *unbalanced* exchange of resources.

Ecological Balance

At this point, I think it important for us to sharpen up the ecological perspective within which we are attempting to evaluate the conceptual components of 'economics'. Whilst initially discussing humankind's attempt to conceptualize, I stressed that this attempt had involved humankind in assuming that it was *separable* from its own existence, and from this Earthly environment; this was in spite of the fact that humankind is part of an ecologically *cohesive* reality.

Subsequently, I attempted to depict how, from an ecological point of view, the global 'ownership' of resources has resulted in an attempt to *separate* the majority of humankind from its resource-base; a humankind which is, once again, part of an ecologically *cohesive* global ecosystem.

In recent pages, however, I have been emphasizing that the evolution of the practice of exchange has resulted in systems that instil relative *imbalance* into the distribution of resources amongst members of the human family. But the ecological significance of this assertion only becomes clear when it is remembered that *balance* is one of the great, qualitative corner-stones of our ecological Universe. The entirety of ecological existence is a dynamic, self-balancing system. From the subatomic to the galactic, all components of our Universe are imbued with a self-balancing capability that occurs, 'of itself'.

Universal energy manifests itself, indeed can only manifest itself, in movement and pulsation. But in being infinitely cohesive, all its movement and pulsation is felt by all the rest of the energy in the Universe. Ultimately, energy's movement and pulsation comes back to move and be felt by itself. And from out of this fact comes Universal *balance*.

Energy's every up, causes a down; every action, a reaction; every emptying, a filling; every clockwise, an anti-clockwise, etc. Cohesion courts balance, and since the Universe's energy coheres, it also *balances*.

Thus, for example, here on Earth our hydrological cycle – involving the precipitation of rain, the flow of water over land masses, the occurrence of the oceans, the evaporation of water from the oceans, cloud formation, and the precipitation of rain once again – is a *balanced* cycle of water movement. The metabolism of materials in the cells of any living organism involves the *balanced*, cyclic interaction of proteins, carbohydrates and enzymes etc.; human blood circulation involves a *balanced* cycle of blood pressures; and in our solar system, the elliptical pathway of the planets about the Sun involves a *balanced* system of interacting forces.

Throughout Nature, and throughout ecological existence, balance manifests itself as an intrinsic ecological quality; and as a part of Nature, humankind's own existence is inexorably self-balancing.

If we now return to our depiction of humankind's emergent conceptualized attempt to instil increasing relative *imbalance* into its resource-exchanges, and view this attempt against the backcloth we have just painted of our self-balancing ecological reality, then we begin to see the ecological inappropriateness of the endeavour. However, by allowing the practice of the unbalanced exchange of resources to mature into the doctrine of the profit-motive, a now conceptualizing humankind showed itself prepared to undertake this endeavour.

Profit: a doctrine of imbalance

In the ecological reality of which humankind is a part, when any resource is moved from one place in an ecosystem to another, then the place from which it is extracted (let us call it location A) 'loses' something or 'gives something up', whilst the place to which it is moved (let us call it location B) 'gains' something or becomes relatively rich in resources. In the Earth's ecosystem, as throughout the Universe, it is only possible for one component to 'gain', when some other component 'loses'.

Thus to think that 'taking' can be undertaken on its own, without any 'giving' elsewhere in the ecosystem, means that only half of the ecological equation is being considered, and such an attitude belies a sort of 'half-blindness':

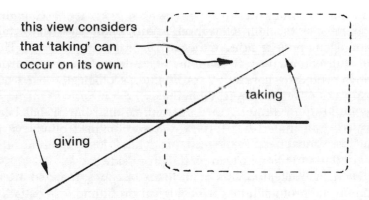

Viewing the entirety of the ecological situation, however, shows that only take *and* give exists – that is, in an ecological reality, only *balance* exists.

This means that when balanced exchanges of resources occurred, then – applying the terms we are currently using – 'loss' and 'gain' were made to equate with one another. When, however, the concept of the unbalanced exchange of resources took root, and matured into the profit-motive, it brought with it the notion that it was possible to take *more* than was given in return, and that it was alright to keep on doing so. This presents us with an opportunity for proposing an *ecological* definition for the concept of the profit-motive:

In ecological terms, the profit-motive insists
that in any exchange of resources
the attempt should be made
to 'take' just a tiny bit more than you 'give'.

However, as I have said, in ecological reality for every tiny bit more taken, there always has to be a tiny bit more given, so it was ecologically inevitable that, over time, the implementation of the profit-motive would result in the build-up of an *imbalance* in the distribution of resources amongst the various human communities.

The resultant imbalance might show itself in the person standing in front of you with whom you are exchanging resources; or it might show itself in the trade statistics of two nations on opposite sides of the world; or it might show itself in the nutrient balance-sheet of an agricultural ecosystem from which you are harvesting profitable, ecologically excessive quantities of nutrients etc. Nonetheless, the intuitive sensing of the build-up of an imbalance in resource-distribution has been denied; humankind has turned a conceptualized blind eye to the loss side of the ecological profit and loss equation, and focused its attention instead on the profit side.

Over the millennia, this main focus of conceptualized attention on the profit-side of the ecological profit and loss equation has matured into a global idolatry. The 'tiny bit more taken' is now enshrined in the concept of profit, and the homage which is paid to it is so ubiquitous and omnipotent that almost all human activity is infused with it.

More important in ecological terms, however, and in terms of our diagram, is the fact that as profit is being made, the 'give – take' line is effectively being *pulled round* about its pivot point, into ever more extreme positions of ecological imbalance. It is from an appreciation of this effect that the term 'profit-pull' has evolved:

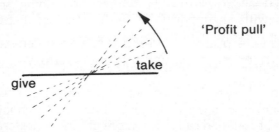

'Profit pull'

The thrust for taking a tiny bit more than is given – the drive to make profit – incessantly *pulls* the ecological distribution of resources into ever more extreme states of imbalance.

What makes this pull incessant is that the making of the first morsel of profit, no matter how small, tends to place the profit-maker in a privileged stance in any subsequent exchange of resources, and a one-way snowball effect is generated.

It is as a reaction to this type of momentum, for example, that the 'UN Convention on the Law of the Sea' has been set up. Thus, in *The Times* dated 5 December, 1984:

> The UN convention of the Law of the Sea has been open for signature for two years... The mineral wealth of the deep sea-bed (copper, nickel nodules etc.) was no sooner fully estimated than it was declared, in a florid phrase: 'the common heritage of mankind'. The concept was adopted by the UN. It (the Convention) means those capable of raising the nodules to the surface should not sail away with the entire benefit from doing so; the benefit is to be spread; and for that, some international, regulatory authority is required.

The UN Convention is clearly reacting to the fact that powerful, already-industrialized countries are claiming *more* than a fair share of ocean-bed resources. That is, they are using their previously won profits to facilitate new profit-making, on the basis that they will be providing most of the advanced technologies for harvesting the sea-bed resources. The perception that the industrialized countries' virtual monopoly over such technologies results from their *already* having more resources than they actually need for ecological survival and well-being is smothered, and instead is used as the basis for their argument that they should get *still more* resources than resource-poor countries elsewhere on the globe.

The Middle Ground, in which you can be content with 'enough', is Forbidden Territory

Today, in our conceptualized, economic world, we can see that 'enough' is never enough; that 'contentment with enough' is dubbed 'lack of ambition'; and that 'more' is always better. Over time, the result is that fewer and fewer human beings are allowed to remain in the common ground in the middle, where a 'sufficiency' permits both ecological contentment and sustainability. Consequently, almost everybody is driven out to the extremities, into being either discontent with 'more than enough' or discontent with 'less than enough'.

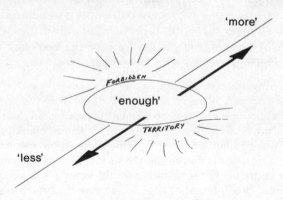

But in the ecological reality of which we are a part, 'enough' is, in fact, optimal, as we shall see later, in ensuring both our current ecological survival and contentment *and* our ecological sustainability.

Over countless aeons
the Universe has sparkled
With countless billions of stars.
One,
our glorious Sun,
warms
pin-point planet Earth,
and Humankind too,
as we walk on her fragile shell.
Her soil and air
fill us
with all the nectars and freshnesses we need
for a beautiful sufficiency;

and all we do is fratch,
over who shall have all,
and who shall have none.

Evidence for the historical existence of the 'profit-pull' effect can be seen in microcosm within the various 'developed' socio-economic systems of the world. Thus in 1984, for example, in the United Kingdom, the most wealthy 50 per cent of the population owned 93 percent of the wealth; and conversely therefore, the remaining 50 per cent owned only 7 per cent. This information was given in the HMSO publication, *Social Trends*, published in 1987, as reported by Andrew Veitch in the *Guardian* on 29 January 1987:

Table 1. Population, Total and Per Capita Gross Domestic Product

	000's	%	$m.	%	$ per capita
World	4,591,463	100.0	11,015,213	100.0	2,399
Developed Countries	802,578	17.5	7,691,135	69.8	9,583
Developing Countries	2,326,155	50.7	2,077,174	18.9	893
Socialist – Europe	383,298	8.3	1,001,229+	9.1	2,612
Socialist – Asia	1,078,926	23.5	245,681	2.2	228

+ net material product

Source: Handbook of International Trade and Development Statistics 1985 Supplement (UNCATD)

The growth of inequality is analysed for Social Trends by Professor J. H. Halsey, director of social and administrative studies at Oxford...

Professor Halsey says: 'A pattern has emerged of a more unequal society, as between a majority in secure attachment to a still prosperous country and a minority in marginal economic and social conditions.'

Discussion on the March 1989 UK Budget similarly reveals gross imbalances in income distribution. The Guardian's Economics Editor, Christopher Huhne, wrote on 8 March 1989:

My only plea, in what should of necessity be a dismal budget, is that the Chancellor should distribute the burden on to the broadest shoulders. There has been a sharp widening of the gap between rich and poor during the Thatcher years, reversing the trend since the inter-war years. The unequal incidence of unemployment on the unskilled has meant that gross earnings for the bottom 10 per cent of income distribution have increased in real terms by 11 per cent since 1978–9, but the equivalent for the top 10 per cent is 69 per cent.

The tax system has also become less progressive. In his useful new book on the tax system [*Changing Tax: How the System Works and How to Change It, 1989*], John Hills calculates, on the basis of the latest official figures for income distribution (for 1985), that real incomes grew by 7 per cent since 1979, but that the share of the total for the poorest fifth fell from 6.1 per cent to 5.6 per cent. 'This suggests' he argues, 'that their real income after allowing for all taxes and cash benefits fell by 2 per cent between 1979 and 1985: despite economic growth, the poorest were worse off in absolute as well as relative terms.'

In being a long-established free market economy, the UK's commercial activity is profit-oriented. The results of the long-term workings of such an economy, as indicated by the statistics above, clearly substantiate the assertion that the profit-motive (and hence 'profit-pull') is indeed a harbinger of *imbalance* in the distribution of resources amongst members of any given human community.

The same sort of evidence is available at a global level. Table 2 (overleaf) shows the distribution of the world's productive capacity between the industrialized North and the 'developing' or 'under-developed' south. From this we can see that the industrialized countries, with only 17.5 per cent of the world's population, controlled 69.8 per cent of world production in 1982; whilst the 'developing' countries, including socialist Asia, representing 74. 2 per cent of the world's population, controlled only 21.1 per cent of world production.

In terms of the distribution of the Earth's resources amongst members of the human family and their utilization to ensure our continued survival, this situation indicates the extent to which the industrialized, developed North has allowed itself to forget that its disproportionate 'gain', its high gross domestic product, and its impressive economic growth, have all had to

Table 2. Population, and Total and Per Capita Gross Domestic Product

	1982 Population		GDP		
	000's	%	Millon $	%	$ per capita
World	4,591,463	100.0	11,015,213	100.0	2399
Developed Countries	802,578	17.5	7,691,135	69.8	9583
Developing Countries	2,326,155	50.7	2,077,174	18.9	893
Socialist-Europe	383,298	8.3	1,001,229 *	9.1	2612
Socialist-Asia	1,078,926	23.5	245,681	2.2	228

* Net material product.

Source: Handbook of International Trade and Development Statistics, 1985, Supplement (UNCTAD).

come from somewhere; and that somewhere is the Earth's *one* pool of resources, upon which the developing South *also* relies for its sustenance.

Therefore the disproportionate 'gain', for which the developed North is currently praising itself, can only have been won *at the expense of* the disproportionate 'loss' which the under-developed South is currently suffering. North and South are inextricably linked in their common use of the Earth's resource base. Thus if the South were suddenly to start to use its proportionate share of the Earth's resources, this would clearly have a radical impact on the level of functioning of the industrialized North. On this Earth, there is only *one* resource-base from which we must *all* take our resources.

This fundamental ecological fact has been persistently and resolutely ignored, because in attempting to conceptualize its activity, humankind has allowed itself the convenient assumption that 'taking' is *separable* from 'giving'; that what one sector of humankind does is separable from what another sector of humankind experiences; and that what one part of humankind takes from our one Earthly resource-base is separable from and therefore has no impact upon what is left for the rest of humankind. However, as asserted earlier, the ecological reality of which we are a part is cohesive. For every 'take' there *is* a 'give', and for every 'profit' there *is* a 'loss'. And as a consequence of several thousands of years of emergent, and ultimately profit-oriented, economic activity, a relative imbalance in the distribution of resources amongst members of the human family has resulted.

'Profit-pull' and Ecological Sustainability

One component of the balanced functioning of the Earth's ecosystems is the balance which asserts itself between the short-term rate of ultilization of materials and resources, and their long-term rate of utilization. Though variable, an ecologically undistorted ecosystem will, of its own accord, establish a rate of functioning at which its current utilization of resources will *balance* with their long-term availability. Thus, overall, the chances for the sustainability of that ecosystem are optimized.

However, the 'economic' utilization of resources from an ecosystem, being profit-oriented, is consistently taking *more* from that ecosystem than it gives back in return (for example, the American First Bowl experience), or is taking more than the ecosystem can regenerate per unit of time (for example, the world's current exploitation of fossil fuel reserves).

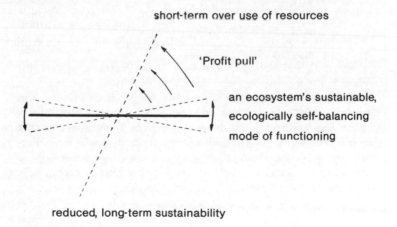

short-term over use of resources

'Profit pull'

an ecosystem's sustainable, ecologically self-balancing mode of functioning

reduced, long-term sustainability

The result of this is that as the economic rate of utilization of resources begins to outstrip the short-term, ecologically optimal rate of utilization, the balance between the short-term and long-term rates of utilization is disrupted, and in this way, the ecological sustainability of the ecosystem begins to be undermined.

Let us look at an African example of this phenomenon, as depicted in Lester Brown's *State of the World – 1986* from the Worldwatch Institute in Washington:

Profiles of Ecological Decline

Accumulating evidence from ecology, agronomy, and hydrology indicates that *sustained over-use of biological systems* can set in motion changes that are self-reinforcing. Each stage of deterioration hastens the onset of the next. When destructive ecological change is coupled with rapid human population growth in subsistence economies, the stage for human tragedy is set.

World Bank energy analyst and ecologist Kenneth Newcombe has described ['An economic justification for rural afforestation: The case for Ethiopia'. Energy Dept. Paper No. 16. World Bank, Washington DC, 1984] how complex, interrelated systems unravel through several stages. His model, based on fieldwork in Ethiopia, portrays a cascading decline in biological and economic productivity triggered by loss of tree cover. According to Newcombe, as people seek new agricultural land, natural forests retreat before the plow. Without trees, mineral nutrients are no longer recycled from deep soil layers. As this nutrient cycle is breached, soil fertility begins to decline. In this first stage, wood supplies remain sufficient and the gradual erosion of cropland fertility is imperceptible.

As rural and village populations grow, markets appear for wood, both for construction and for household fuels. Cutting wood from remnant forests generates income for peasant families, who generally burn crop residues and animal dung in their own households. This in turn interrupts two more nutrient cycles: removing crop residues and diverting dung from fields degrades soil structure and leaves the land more vulnerable to erosion. On sloping fields, annual soil erosion of 50 – 100 tons per hectare is common. The depletion of remaining forests then accelerates, and the loss of soil fertility begins to reduce crop yields.

Once nearby stands of trees are gone, dung and crop residues turn up in local markets where formerly only wood was sold. The steady loss of nutrients and organic matter from croplands severely limits crop yields and the ability of pastures to support livestock. A greater share of family cash income comes from the sale of dung than from that of food crops, for erratic crop yields prove barely sufficient even for subsistence.

Eventually, cow dung becomes the main fuel source in villages and thus the main cash crop from nearby farms. Rural families use crop residues for cooking and as fodder for their livestock, which can no longer be supported by grazing land. Pervasive topsoil depletion leaves farmers vulnerable to total crop failure during even routine dry seasons. In markets, both food and fuel prices rise rapidly.

When this final stage is reached in a subsistence economy, biological productivity is destined to collapse. Families can no longer produce enough food for themselves or their livestock, let alone for markets. A massive exodus from rural areas begins, often triggered by drought that could formerly have been tolerated. Famine is widespread; peasants' lack of purchasing power is compounded by absolute shortages of food at any price.

This model of an accelerating cycle of degradation is now being confirmed in portions of Africa. A joint UN Development Program/World Bank report points out that 'this transition from the first to the final stage is in process right across Ethiopia and has reached the terminal phase in parts of Tigre and Eritrea. [United Nations Development Program/World Bank Energy Sector Assessment Program, 'Ethiopia: Issues and Options in the Energy Sector'. World Bank, Washington, DC, 1984]. At a World Bank workshop in Botswana in March 1985, Newcombe warned 'There is evidence that (the final stage) has already been reached in some areas of several countries in Southern Africa and that virtually every country has areas that have reached (the point at which wood gathering has overtaken land clearing as a cause of deforestation) [Kenneth Newcombe, 'Household energy supply: The energy crisis that is here to stay!' presented to the World Bank Senior Policy Seminar – Energy, Gabarone, Botswana, 18–22, March 1985].

The cascading effect Newcombe describes results from disruption of the self-regulating mechanisms of natural systems on which humans depend.

97

At each stage in this monitored descent into ecological dissolution, the balanced functioning of, in this instance, Ethiopia's ecosystems, is systematically being abused, and ultimately destroyed.

The question I should like to ask, with regard to this cited example of ecological degeneration is 'Why?' Why is there sustained overuse of biological systems? Why do people seek new agricultural land? Why is there disruption of the self-regulating mechanisms of natural systems on which humans depend?

The answer, I believe, is that today's economic system is global in its impact, and all-pervasive in its influence. It thus even affects rural African exchanges of resources, and as already discussed, in being profit-oriented, it perpetually insists that just a little bit more is taken from the ecosystems on which it is based than is given back in return. The global economic system insists that, for example, timber is extracted faster than it can be regenerated, it insists that more nutrients are taken out of the soil than are put back in, it insists that ecological structure and organization is disrupted, without allowing time for its repair.

Thus, as this Ethiopian example shows, an 'economic' humankind currently seeks to *profit* from the ecosystems themselves, on which it relies for its survival. But in so doing, it disrupts the *balance* between such ecosystems' short-term and long-term utilization of resources, with the result that their ecological sustainability is ultimately destroyed.

A second example of this effect is illustrated by the following newspaper article by John Gribbin (*The Guardian*, 5 April 1988), dealing with the profit-oriented production of chloro-fluoro-carbons (CFCs) and the disruption of our atmosphere's balanced production of ozone:

Danger Zones

Springtime depletion of ozone in the Antarctic stratosphere, now an annual event, may have repercussions across the southern hemisphere and beyond. Some observations suggest that ozone from far outside Antarctica is draining into the 'hole' over

Antarctica in southern summer, with resulting increases in ultra-violet radiation at ground level in southern South America, Australia and New Zealand...

Ozone is constantly being manufactured and constantly being destroyed, by natural processes in the atmosphere. The natural balance is a bit like the way the water level stays constant in a bath being filled by water from a tap and drained from a hole in the bottom. If the hole is made a bit bigger, water squirts out in a rush and the level in the bath drops. But as the level drops, the pressure eases until inflow and outflow are again in balance, at a lower level.

Because of the hole in the ozone layer over Antarctica, the balance over the southern hemisphere has tilted sufficiently to cause a reduction in ozone concentrations, according to recent calculations, of about 4 per cent over the whole southern stratosphere...

But the most important lesson now being drawn from the hole over Antarctica is that the world's atmospheric system does indeed include sensitive balance points, where human activities that seem unimportant when averaged over the whole globe can trigger dramatic, and perhaps irreversible, changes. A point to ponder, the next time you are offered coffee in a styrofoam cup that has been 'foamed' with the aid of CFCs.

The entirety of the world's climatic system is a coherent process, which itself meshes in with all the world's surface ecosystems, and with the rate of incoming energy from the Sun. Its functioning is in a fine balance, and as part of that functioning, ozone is produced in the stratosphere at a given rate. The production of ozone destroying CFCs, at a rate *within* the rate of natural, ozone replenishment could therefore be accomodated, but since CFC manufacture is profit-orientated, ever greater quantities are produced, with the result that the balance between ozone production and ozone depletion is upset. This is just one example of millions of processes in which the profit-oriented use of resources is instilling *imbalance* into the functioning of our ecosystems.

It is therefore reasonable for us to conclude that profit-oriented industry and commerce, and hence 'profit-pull', is instrumental in creating conditions of imbalance, not only in the distribution of resources amongst human beings, but also in the functioning of the ecosystems on which humankind relies for its survival. As a consequence, the ecological sustainability of these ecosystems is being seriously undermined.

No Ecologically Meaningful Basis for *Employment*

Over the millennia the unbalanced exchange of resources, and subsequently the profit-oriented exchange of resources, have resulted, as previously discussed, in the development of an extreme imbalance in the global distribution and ownership of resources. In the world today there is a minority of resource-rich people, and a majority of effectively resourceless people.

We have previously cited the situation in the UK where, in 1984, the wealthiest 50 per cent of the population owned 93 per cent of the wealth, whilst the poorest 50 per cent owned only 7 per cent. In Costa Rica the situation is even more extreme, and in a *Guardian* article entitled 'The Land Stand' (6 April 1984), Jonathon Steel indicated the degree of resourcelessness, by referring to the number of landless people in the country:

> No one knows for sure how many Costa Ricans can be described as 'landless', or would go back to the land if it became available. The rural unions list at least 3,000 families, but Ricardo Zeledon, the director of post-graduate studies in Agrarian Law, at the University of Costa Rica, estimates the number on closer to 200,000 people (in a nation of 2,500,00).

Similarly in Brazil the degree of effective resourcelessness, as indicated by the number of landless 'peasants', has reached amazing proportions. In a *Guardian* article by Jan Jocha from Sao Paulo (16 May 1984), about the eviction of 1,000 landless squatters from 21,000 acres of unused land, reference is made to Brazil's estimated 12 million landless families.

Brazilian Landless Squatters Evicted

> A thousand peasants who had occupied empty land in the south of Mato Grosso state, 500 miles from Sao Paulo, have been evicted in a large-scale police operation. Two weeks ago they

occupied a 21,000 acre area claimed but never used by a local company. The company, Somerco, then obtained a court eviction order, although the peasants allege that it has not proved its ownership of the area...

The police tore down the tents and moved them out, ignoring the appeals of the local Catholic mission and dozens of priests and nuns, who have been supporting the peasants' claim to a piece of land to grow food for their families...

Crowded into lorries, the peasants were driven away. Nine hundred of them have now camped in the church in Izinhema, a small town 80 miles away.

This was the biggest land occupation in recent years, and is seen as a sign of the growing organisation of the landless peasants, believed to number 12 million families throughout Brazil.

The peasants who occupied the land near Izinhema came from the southern states, where they worked as seasonal rural labourers, after losing their own land. Some of them were driven off by the spread of mechanised soya bean farming, others by the growth of large sugar cane estates to provide alcohol for Brazil's alternative energy programme. Many more lost their lands to government hydro-electric projects, especially the giant Italpu dam on the border with Paraguay. According to Church sources, there are over 100 million acres of empty but fertile land in Brazil.

From this sort of evidence we can see that at some point in our recent evolution the unbalanced and subsequently profit-oriented exchange of resources must have gone so far that some human beings ended up owning virtually no life-essential resources at all, whilst other initially resource-rich owners had gone on to own resources way in excess of anything they could ever process themselves. The recognition of this imbalance is significant enough in its own right, but it appears even more significant when it is viewed in the context of what it subsequently facilitated, because it was this self-same imbalance, I believe, which led to the conceptualization and institutionalization of human 'employment'.

In the introductory section on Ownership, I demonstrated that every human being is an ecological component of the Earth's ecological system. On this basis, I went on to say that

101

every human being has the need to consume an ecologically determined 'sufficiency' of resources in order to survive. For this purpose, human communities are endowed with an ecologically determined capability to 'hunt or gather' and thereby obtain that sufficiency of resources; and in an ecologically undistorted situation, human beings would have been busy obtaining that sufficiency from the ecological environment of which they were a part.

The factor which underpins this situation is the one stated at the beginning and the end of the paragraph above – every human being is *part of* the Earth's ecosystem and hence is *part of* the habitat in which he or she exists. As such, resources, if available at all in that habitat, are immediately, unconceptualizedly and uncontestedly available for every human being to busy herself or himself upon, so that she or he can consume them up to the level of their need, and thereby survive. That is, it is the immediate, unconceptualized, uncontested *availability* of needed resources, which furnishes the situation in which every human being can be *busy* procuring those needed resources.

However, in the situation characterized by an extreme imbalance in the ownership of resources, it began to occur that some people ended up with no resources freely available to them. In this predicament, such people no longer had any resources immediately, unconceptualizedly and uncontestedly *available* to them, on which to *busy* themselves. Effectively, they had been made **resourceless**.

It was at this point, and *only* at this point, I would suggest, that human beings first became **employable**.

It is only *after* ecological human beings have had the resources of which they are a part 'owned away' from them; it is only *after* ecological human beings have been effectively separated from the resource-base of which they are a part; it is only *after* ecological human beings have been made effectively resourceless through the development of an extreme imbalance in resource ownership, that they become employable and can be **employed**. And it is only after the development of the same imbalance in the ownership of resources, that resource-rich

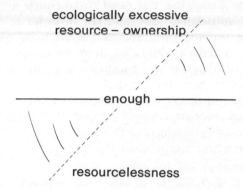

owners have an excess of resources on which work needs to be done, and hence have the **employment** to give to '**employable** ' people.

The fact that the resource-rich owners have an *excess* of resources – that is more than they can cope with and process themselves – becomes the reason why they require human labour, when in ecological reality, the people who really need assistance are those with less than the sufficiency they require to ensure their survival.

In simple terms, therefore, we can say that resulting from an extreme *imbalance* in resource ownership, the twin phenomena of 'resourcelessness' and 'excessive resource ownership' have been the immediate pre-requisites for the creation of the concept of 'employment'. And this involves a humankind that is part of an ecologically *self-balancing* reality.

Underpinning all this, however, 'ownership' has been the conceptual lever with which, by today, a large proportion of humankind has been effectively *separated from* and prised away from its resource-base and made resourceless. Thus, I believe, we can now identify six levels at which the attempt has been made to consolidate the initial attempt to dislocate a large proportion of humankind from the resource-base of which it is a part:

The initial attempt to dislocate: the application of the concept of ownership, with its essential assumption of separability.

103

First level: human beings made 'resourceless' through an extreme imbalance in resource-ownership.

Second level: such human beings made 'employable' through having been made resourceless.

Third level: such employable human beings being 'employed' by the owners of ecologically excessive amounts of resource on which work needed to be done.

Fourth level: such excessively resource-rich owners becoming recognized as 'employers'.

Fifth level: such resourceless, employed people becoming recognized as 'employees'.

Sixth level: such work, done by employees, on resources owned by employers, being institutionalized as 'employment'.

Hundreds of millions of now 'resourceless' human beings around the world no longer have any life-essential resources immediately, unconceptualizedly and uncontestably available to them, upon which they can be 'busy' in order to sustain themselves. Fundamentally, therefore, what 'employment' really gives them, what a 'job' actually gives these millions of resourceless people, is *resources* to 'busy' themselves upon – that's all. In this way we can see that the ownership of resources has conferred upon resource-owners the authority to give to, or to take from resourceless people, the 'opportunity to work', and that this is based on their being able to give resources to, or to take resources from, resourceless people, at will.

Yet, resources are not anybody's to give. In ecological reality, *every* human being on Earth can never be anything other than 'resourced', because we are all incontestably a part of this Earth's resource-base. Therefore I maintain that there is no ecologically meaningful basis for employment.

***

On the basis of this ecological evaluation, not only is it possible to show that employment is founded on the ecological impossibility of the dislocation of humankind from its resource-base, but it is also possible to show that once institutionalized, the employment of human labour actually provides the energy to make the situation progressively worse.

Let us consider a hypothetical country in which the concept of ownership has been established for several generations. All the country's resources have been taken into ownership by, shall we say, 30 per cent of the adult population, whilst the remaining 70 per cent are resourceless and are employed to work on those owned resources. This work will be performed according to the dictates of the owners, and tradeable resources will result. These resources will then be exchanged in market transactions between owner-employers and employees, and in the competitive situation which prevails, some owner-employers will lose market-share, whilst others will gain market-share. For the owners who gain by their transactions, their reward will be increased financial power and increased exchange-power; and with this power, such owners will be able to increase their ownership of resources.

Thus, the work put in by the already-resourceless, employed population, merely provides the energy for the mechanism by which owners compete with one another. Some win, some lose; and the owners who 'win' stand to increase their share of resource-ownership. The result is that even amongst themselves, fewer and fewer owners end up owning the resources, and people who once owned resources swell the ranks of the resourceless.

Hence we can say that whilst resourcelessness is the pre-requisite for employment, once established, employment exacerbates resourcelessness.

***

And whilst a great deal of intellectual energy is currently expended upon the problem of 'employment', almost none is applied to the more fundamental problem of the global 'resource-lessness', upon which employment is based. In view of this, we might be forgiven for concluding that, in effect, 'employment' is being used as an anaesthetic, to mitigate the pain that enforced human 'resourcelessness' is currently causing humankind.

Today's Population Explosion is Caused by 'Economics'

The effective separation of the majority of humankind from its resource-base brought about by ownership, and the subsequent imbalance in the distribution of resources created by profit-oriented economics are, I believe, the twin factors that are causing our current human population explosion. In his book *The Turning Point* (1982), Fritjof Capra outlines the now-established demographic argument that population growth stabilizes when social and economic improvement in any given country is sufficient to result in the reduction of *both* death-rate *and* birth-rate, and that globally this will only occur when the 'benefits' of our worldwide industrial and economic activity are more evenly distributed to *all* members of the human family:

> The Influence of Cartesian – Newtonian Thought, and The Impasse of Economics

> To slow down the rapid depletion of our natural resources we need not only to abandon the idea of continuing economic growth, but to control the worldwide increase in population. The dangers of this 'population explosion' are now generally recognized, but views on how to achieve 'zero population growth' differ widely, with proposed methods ranging from education and voluntary family planning to coercion by legal means and by brute force. Most of these proposals are based on the view of the problem as a purely biological phenomenon, related only to fertility and contraception. But there is now conclusive evidence, collected by demographers around the world, that population growth is affected as much, if not more, by powerful social factors. The view that this research demands sees the rate of growth as affected by a complex interplay of biological, social and psychological forces [Barry Commoner, 'How poverty breeds over population'. In Arditti, Rita, Brennan, Pat and Cavrak, Steve (eds.) *Science and Liberation*, South End Press, Boston, 1980].

Demographers have discovered that the significant pattern is a transition between two levels of stable populations that has been characteristic of all Western countries. In pre-modern societies birth rates were high, but so were death rates, and thus the population size was stable. As living conditions improved during the time of the Industrial Revolution, death rates began to fall, and, with birth rates remaining high, populations increased rapidly. However, with continuing improvement of living standards, and with the decline in death rates continuing, birth rates began to decline as well, thus reducing the rate of population growth. The reason for this decline has now been observed worldwide. Through the interplay of social and psychological forces, the quality of life – the fulfilment of material needs, a sense of well-being, and confidence in the future – becomes a powerful and effective motivation for controlling population growth.

There is, in fact, a critical level of well-being which has been shown to lead to a rapid reduction in birth rate and an approach to a balanced population. Human societies, then, have developed a self-regulating process, based on social conditions, which results in a demographic transition from a balanced population, with high birth rates and high death rates and a low standard of living, to a population with a higher standard of living which is larger but again in balance, and in which both birth and death rates are low.

The present global population crisis is due to the rapid increase of population in the Third World, and the considerations outlined above show clearly that this increase continues because the conditions for the second phase of the demographic transition have not been met. During their colonial past the Third World countries experienced an improvement in living conditions that was sufficient to reduce death rates and thus initiated population growth. But the rise of living standards did not continue, because the wealth generated in the colonies was *diverted* to the developed countries, where it helped their populations to become balanced. This process continues today, as many Third World countries remain colonized in the economic sense. This exploitation continues to increase the affluence of the colonizers and prevents Third World populations from reaching the standard of living conducive to a reduction of their rate of growth.

The world population crisis, then, is an unanticipated effect of international exploitation, a consequence of the fundamental interrelatedness of the global ecosystem, in which every exploitation eventually comes back to haunt the exploiters. From this point of view it becomes quite apparent that ecological balance also requires social justice. The most effective way to control population growth will be to help the people of the Third World achieve a level of well-being that will induce them to limit their fertility voluntarily. This will require a global redistribution of wealth in which some of the world's wealth is returned to the countries that have played a major role in producing it.

An important aspect of the population problem, which is not generally known, is that the cost of bringing the standard of living of poor countries to a level that appears to convince people that they should not have excessive numbers of children is very small compared to the wealth of developed countries. That is to say, there is enough wealth to support the entire world at a level that leads to a balanced population. The problem is that this wealth is unevenly distributed...

A similar conclusion is reached in the report from the World Commission on Environment and Development entitled *Our Common Future* (1987, p. 106):

Poverty breeds high rates of population growth: Families poor in income, employment, and social security need children first to work and later to sustain elderly parents. Measures to provide an adequate livelihood for poor households, to establish and enforce minimum-age child labour laws, and to provide publicly financed social security will all lower fertility rates. Improved public health and child nutrition programmes that bring down infant mortality rates – so parents do not need 'extra' children as insurance against child death – can also help to reduce fertility levels.

All these programmes are effective in bringing down birth rates only when their benefits are shared by the majority. Societies that attempt to spread the benefits of economic growth to a wider segment of the population may do better at lowering birth rates than societies with both faster and higher levels of economic growth but a less even sharing of the benefits of that growth.

I agree with this conclusion, but would add that an equitable distribution of resources to all parts of the human family will be impossible to achieve using any 'economic' mechanism. Any economic system based, as ours is, on the ownership of resources, the *'more* ethic', unbalanced, profit-oriented systems of exchange, and employment, brings with it the *inevitability* that an imbalance in the distribution of resources will result; and, as asserted in the excerpts above, it is the current *imbalance* in the global distribution of resources that is the root cause of today's global population explosion.

Whilst over thousands of years we have shown ourselves ready to create relative imbalance in the functioning of the ecosystems from which we take our resources, we have also assumed our separability from, and hence immunity from, the consequences of such activity. But in an ecologically cohesive world, there can be no complete immunity from anything. Consequently the relative imbalance we have created in the distribution of our resources is now coming home to roost in the form of ecologically unbalanced rates of growth in our own human population.

Up to now, in our discussion of one of the most globally influential consequences of humankind's attempt to lead a conceptualized existence – namely, today's economic system – we have highlighted important instances where that system has attempted to instil effective separation and imbalance into an ecological reality characterized by cohesion and balance. In the sections which follow, consideration will be given to the related ecological factors of energy, rate of functioning, and energy-efficiency, before returning once again to a final consideration of humankind's assumption of separability in the pursuance of its conceptualized economic lifestyle.

To set the scene for these sections, we need to refer, though only very briefly, to humankind's recent advances in science and technology, because it is these that have unlocked the flood of additional energy, which 'economic' humankind currently has at its disposal.

Energy to our Elbow

It is not intended to incorporate a detailed ecological assessment of scientific or technological methodology in this work. Suffice it to say, however, that the basic flaw which is intrinsic in all human attempts to conceptualize is also present in all conceptualized, scientific and technological methodology. Underpinning all scientific observation is the assumption that the human observer can completely separate himself or herself from the object under investigation.

Thus, for example, in the Cartesian mode of investigation, the observer assumes that all his or her observations are meaningfully objective; that his or her influence on the subject matter, whilst conducting the observations, can be actually detached from, and hence excluded from, the course of the observations being made. Similarly, it is thought acceptable that ecological factors which are considered peripheral to the specific subject under study, can be cut off and moved out of the range of consideration, without detriment to the validity of the observations made.

In addition, the components of the study-material are identified and dissembled, so that at the most fundamental level the investigation involves a consideration of fragments of what was previously a cohesively functioning entity. And subsequent research usually involves an effort to determine how these fragments might have worked together had they been left intact. In an ecologically cohesive reality, no such 'fragments' exist.

For example, there is no such discrete subject as physiology. Animals' bodies do function, but they do so as part of, and in total synchronization with, everything else in their environment, and hence in the Universe. Physiology is not separately identifiable from, for example, psychology, meteorology or geology etc.; it coheres and interacts with all of these, and with everything else.

This is essentially a mundane re-statement of the 'Heisenberg Uncertainty Principle', in which Heisenberg said that it was not possible to determine an electron's position *and* speed around the atomic nucleus simultaneously; that only one factor *or* the other could be determined at any one time. That is, Heisenberg acknowledged that scientific study has to assume the separability of the material under observation. (See, for example, *Chemistry*, by Pauling and Pauling, 1975)

Nonetheless, one of the consequences which has resulted from humankind's conceptualized scientific and technological endeavours is its procurement of extra sources of energy. These represent absolutely additional supplies to humankind's own store of energy-- that is, distilled-off, separated-out, controllable amounts of additional energy.

***

Human labour, and increasingly *employed* human labour, together with animal draught-power, and wind- and water-power, provided the energy whereby owned resources were processed for consumption, when the manipulation of the human environment was in its infancy. This was broadly the case right up until the advent of the cottage industries. Subsequently, however, with the discovery of coal and its utilization in the production of steam-power, the era dawned in which such energy sources were to be superseded. Steam-power gave the process of mechanization a profound boost, and the technological revolution which resulted facilitated the discovery of oil. Today coal, oil, petrol, gas and uranium provide most of the energy which drives the global mechanization with which we are so familiar.

The discovery of such enormous quantities of fossil energy and the mechanization it facilitated instigated a plethora of significant developments. For example, the massive injection of fossil-fuel energy into the ecosystems on which we rely, together with the mechanised monitoring of time, has influenced the *rate* at which humankind has attempted to experience its conceptualized existence. We can also note the emergence of industrialized societies, with their extended manufacturing processes, increased opportunities for profit-making, their accelerated demand for resources, and their specializations. More recently, the development of advanced mechanization and computerization has resulted in a reduction in the demand for human labour and skills, and hence to an increase in human 'unemployment'.

At a fundamental level, all these and many other developments that characterize modern, economic, industrialized societies, have been brought about, I believe, by the increased availability of hitherto unknown quantities of usable energy. I should like to proceed therefore, to a consideration of some of these developments.

In what is an ecologically oriented analysis, this is, I believe, a reasonable proposition since a consideration of energy and the level and manner of its utilization is one of the most basic studies we can undertake.

Time, Rate and Acceleration

The flow of the Universe, the movement of the stars, the turning of the solar system, the weights, the distances between and the orbiting speeds of the components of the solar system, give the Earth we inhabit its 'event-occurrences' and its periodicities: the solar year, our lunar month, our morning, noon and night, etc. As Earthly inhabitants, our own existence is infused with this flow of event-occurrences and periodicities:

- the turning of the year gives us our seasons of lean and plenty;
- the waxing and waning of the month gives us our cycles of fertility; and
- the turning of the day gives us our patterns of sleeping and waking etc.

These event-occurrences and periodicities give our existence feature and form, just as the movement of the stars and the turning of the galaxies give feature and form to the otherwise featureless passage of Universal Time.

And for humankind all this was fine, and as it should have been, until, that is, humankind began to make the effort to conceptualize, and in particular, for the purposes of this chapter, until humankind began to make the effort to conceptualize Universal Time. This involved us in the attempt to *step back from* the flowing of these event-occurrences and periodicities that are, in ecological reality, part of our very experiencing of existence. It involved us in assuming a separation from them, so that we could claim to be getting an accurate and meaningful 'view' of them, and hence give them conceptualized descriptions and titles, such as year, month, day, second, etc.

However, ecologically this was not possible because, as already discussed, the reality of which we are a part is not divisible in this way; it is cohesive, and so our assumption of separability was without ecological foundation. Nonetheless, at some time in its past, humankind did make this assumption and hence we did assume that we could meaningfully conceptualize 'time'.

Initially the conceptualized units of time were used, I believe, to *identify* ecological periodicities that impinged quite directly upon our existence: the waxing and waning of the Moon each 'month'; the four 'seasons' of the year with their distinctive climatic and vegetative characteristics; 'morning' from dawn till noon, and 'afternoon' from noon till sunset etc. But eventually this labelling became a framework of conceptualized intervals, a grid of time-references, *through which* we began to view the flow of the existence going on around us, and the flowing of our *own* existence, as though these were separated from us. In this way, what had once been a means of marking out or describing the flow of our ecological existence, now became a means of monitoring and hence of *timing* that flow.

Thus a certain angle of the Sun at noon was no longer simply an indicator of the occurrence or the flowing or the passing of our year; it was rather that 'every year', the Sun would be at a certain angle at noon. Whereas before, in agricultural settlements, the turning of the year brought the harvest; now the harvest was something which occurred 'each year'. The turning of the year brought repeated spells of hot, sunny weather, but then with the conceptualization and designation of the 'months' of the year, we started to say: In June, July and August we will get hot, sunny weather (in the Northern Hemisphere, that is). Instead of being a means of merely *describing* the occurrence of repeated events, the units of time that were conceptualized became a veritable lattice-work, *through which* events were seen to occur. Thus the emphasis gradually changed so that eventually things were seen to happen in *terms of time*.

It was in appreciation of this conceptual development that Harry Snodgrass Junior mused, on a bright May morning, in 1912: 'I wonder whether this afternoon will still happen if my pocket watch stops'.

'I wonder whether this afternoon will still happen, if my pocket watch stops?'

The significance of detailing all this is that once units of time had been conceptualized and had been used to monitor the flow of events going on around humankind, and also to monitor the flow of humankind's own activity, we had availed ourselves, I believe, of the essential ingredient whereby we could go on to conceptualize *rate*. For in conjunction with the conceptualization of such things as numbers, weights and distances, which facilitate the conceptualization of quantity, we can define rate as 'quantity flowing per unit of time'. We were thus able to say that a certain weight of grain could be harvested from one acre *each year*; that a certain area could be cultivated per person *per day*; that a certain distance could be travelled on foot *in so many hours*, etc.

This meant that in conjunction with the now well-established concept of the *'more* ethic', utilization of the concept of *rate* gave us the conceptual vessel into which extra doses of energy could be injected to give us *acceleration,* and hence accelerated rates of functioning. We now knew things happened at a certain rate, and that things could be done at a certain rate. How could we get *more* out of these ecosystems? How could we *accelerate* these processes? What we needed was more *energy*.

As already stated, human conceptualized effort, and sub-sequently, human labour, animal draught-power, wind-power and water-power etc. provided, I believe, the injections of energy with which the ecosystems on which we relied were initially accelerated. More recently, and by using mechanical, scientific and technological methodologies, the energy sources mentioned earlier – coal, oil, petrol, gas, uranium (and sugar) – have been harnessed and have made hitherto undreamt-of quantities of additional energy available for injection into these ecosystems, facilitating hitherto undreamt-of degrees of accele-ration in their rates of functioning.

But whilst the former sources of additional energy (human labour, animal draught-power, etc.) were, shall we say, 'ecologi-cally-bound' forms of energy, the latter (e.g. electricity from coal etc.) are what we might call 'effectively-separated-out' forms of energy. And what is significant about effectively-separated-out forms of energy is that their re-injection into ecosystems is much less subject to the moderating effects of ecological containment. In having been unhitched from their ecological, evolutionary bearing material or situation, the rein-jection of effectively-separated-out forms of energy into ecosys-tems does not have to conform, to the same extent, to ecological proportionality.

For example, the work-energy you get from a bullock in one day is very much determined by the rate at which it gets physiologically tired. The electricity you derive in one day from a nuclear reactor, on the other hand, whilst still being related to the store of energy bound up in uranium, can nonetheless, once distilled out, be re-applied to other ecosystems, with potentially much less regard for the latter's ecological parameters and rates of functioning. The result is that the energy going round in these energy-injected ecosystems can be *in excess* of their ecological optima. Industrialized humankind has then observed the functioning of these energy-injected systems *through* its latticework of conceptualized units of time, and has been thrilled to find that it has *accelerated* their functioning. From these accelerated systems we have been delighted to take *more* resources per unit of time than would otherwise have been possible: *more* tons of grain per acre per annum; *more* miles travelled per hour; *more* sights seen per human lifetime, etc.

But there are two things that characterize these accelerated systems which, from an ecological point of view, are less delightful, and which I believe we have allowed ourselves to ignore. Firstly, as referred to earlier (p. 95) the boosting of the current or short-term rate of functioning of any ecological system above its ecological un-self-realized optimum necessarily impairs that system's ecological sustainability. This is because the current rate of cycling of an ecosystem's resources and its sustainability are *both* interdependent parts of the overall optimization of that system's functioning, and where the former is forced up, the latter is reduced.

For example, whilst mechanized and fossil-fuel-assisted fishing methods resulted in the accelerated catching of sardines off the US Pacific coast between 1925 and 1935, and anchovies off the Peruvian coast between 1955 and 1970, the sustainability of their respective ecosystems was correspondingly wrecked as a consequence of being overfished. (See *Agricultural Ecology*, 1979, by Cox and Atkins, pp. 572–580.)

Secondly, I believe that we have forgotten that we are still *part of* the ecological systems we have been so avidly trying to accelerate, and that if we inject ecologically excessive quantities of energy into the ecological systems on which we rely and with which our existence is enmeshed, we ultimately infuse ecologically excessive energy into ourselves.

The 'high-powered' lives of people in today's industrialized, energy-intensive societies are characterized by stress-related, degenerative diseases: heart diseases, stomach ulcers, cancer, etc., and these bear witness to the indirect injection of ecologically excessive amounts of supplementary energy into, in this case, the *human* ecosystem. Thus, for example, in Japan stress brought on by the pressures of modern industrialized living has resulted in a dramatic increase in the rate of suicides:

> Business of Death in Japan: Lisa Martineau looks at the rise in suicides among the executive Samurai.
>
> Endaka, the Japanese word for the sharp appreciation of the yen, is being blamed for the deaths this year of 12 Japanese chief executives. Since September 1985, the 70% rise in the value of the yen against the dollar has put pressure on Japanese exporters, who are taking huge losses at home rather than lose market share abroad. The men, mostly in their 50's and 60's, ran big corporations such as All Nippon Airways, Mitsubishi, Kawasaki Steel, and Seiko Epson. The immediate causes of death, in a country where the average life expectancy for males is 75, was anything from pneumonia to heart attacks. But the symptoms of executive malaise run even deeper.
>
> According to the National Police Agency (NPA), last year's record suicide rate included 487 management-level executives – 195 of whom ran manufacturing industries which had been severely affected by Endaka. Comparing 1978 (when figures were first kept) with 1986, the suicide rate for executives has jumped 57 per cent. The highest increase of 103 per cent (comparing 1978 to 1986) is found in the bureaucratic managerial class. Now a suicide prevention manual for civil servants has been used.
>
> Despite the fact that Japan is the second richest country in the world, the NPA says since 1978 the number of suicides caused by economic woes has increased 60 per cent; and those caused by job problems by 50 per cent. The general suicide rate in Japan has been rising over the last three years.
>
> Last year's figure – the highest ever – means there was a suicide every 20 minutes; three times as many deaths a year as in traffic accidents. For people in their 50's, the suicide rate has almost doubled since 1979, caused by 'economic reasons and the stresses of Japan's competitive society,' according to the NPA.
>
> (*The Guardian*, 18 August 1987)

Ultimately, injecting energy into our support-systems accelerates our own experiencing. In this way, people 'pit themselves against time' – that is, against real, ecological time and hence against the real, ecological rate of their own experience of existence – in their attempt to accelerate that experience. But as discussed earlier, humankind is a component of the Earth's ecosystem, and as such it functions, and therefore experiences, at an ecologically optimal rate, and within a given range of variation that rate of experiencing will remain broadly constant. That is, there seems to be a certain amount of experiencing, both qualitative and quantitative, of which we are capable, and whatever we might try to do to alter that amount of experiencing, it will always stay roughly the same.

Thus, whilst we might accelerate the rate at which we live our lives so that we meet more events per unit of conceptualized time, our *qualitative* ability to relish and appreciate that increased number of events declines proportionately. Hence our overall amount of experiencing, comprising both quantitative and qualitative components, will stay roughly the same:

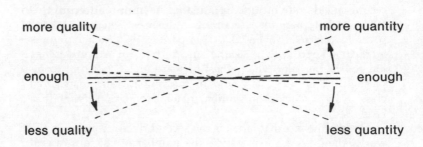

This is not to imply simply that *less* is better. Rather my intention is to imply that in our attempting to live a conceptualized lifestyle, specifically in this instance either a conceptually accelerated or conceptually decelerated lifestyle, we are injecting extra energy into the living of our lives, only to glean roughly the same amount of overall, qualitative and quantitative experiencing from it.

Why is it then that we are perpetually demanding *more* from our lives? Why should acceleration be one of *the* hallmarks of our advanced, economic societies? The answer is, I believe, that in our attempt to create a conceptualized lifestyle, with its concomitant attempt to subjugate the intuitive, we are perpetually precluded from achieving the feelings of satisfaction and contentment which, in ecological reality, are only ever experienced intuitively.

As an example, let us consider the phenomenon of the demand any ecological entity might make for the resources that are essential for its survival. Specifically, let us consider the *intuitive* demand an animal might make for such resources, and then compare this with the *conceptualized* demand a modern human consumer might make.

Intuitive and Conceptualized Demand

When a 'dumb' unconceptualizing animal feels itself to be in need of a thing – for instance, water, shelter or food – it experiences a 'sensation' which is felt internally. Such an animal is capable of sensing a need or a deficit *intuitively*. Without attempting to conceptualize it, the animal actually experiences a feeling inside of needing something, and is thereby driven to do something about it. It seeks out an amount of the resource which it requires – an additional unit of that of which it is currently in need – and consumes it. The animal actually *experiences* the consumption of that additional unit of resource, without it being conceptualized. It might then go on to consume and actually experience the consumption of one more unit of that resource, again without it being conceptualized. Let us assume then, that with the consumption of this second unit of resource, the animal feels, *intuitively*, that it has had enough. At this point, the drive to seek out more resources abates, and the animal perhaps rests from its searching and actually experiences some contentment, at least for a while.

There is, of course, another alternative. The animal could go on and consume a third additional unit of the resource and actually experience that consumption. But if, as we hypothesized above, the consumption of two units of the resource was enough to satisfy its requirements, then with the consumption of this third unit, the animal would experience a feeling of having had 'too much'. Its drive to seek out more resources would abate immediately and it would not feel comfortable or content. It would only feel comfortable and content after it had somehow shed that excess unit of resource.

This depiction of the demand an animal might make on its environment for resources is an example of its *intuitive* sensing mechanism, since it involves intuitive, unconceptualized responses to internally sensed states of: 'need', 'needing more', 'enoughness' or 'insufficiency', and 'too much'. It is its ability to actually experience the sensation of having had 'enough' that allows an animal to sense *not* having had enough, and on the other hand, having had too much of a thing. The converse is also true; it is the ability to experience the sensations of 'not enough' and of 'too much', that enables any ecological entity to feel its way intuitively towards a state of satisfaction and contentment, for a certain length of time.

This intuitive sensing mechanism is a component, and an exceedingly important component, of the predominant type of evolution which has occurred on the Earth and throughout the Universe; namely a completely *unconceptualizing* evolution. As part of an unconceptualizing evolution, an inherently *intuitive* humankind was capable of fully sensing and responding intuitively to a 'deficit', an 'excess' and a 'sufficiency' of resources in just this way. Humankind functioned intuitively and undertook activity up to the point at which its real ecological needs were satisfied, and then it rested and could experience contentment for a time. We have a recent example of this in the North American Indians:

Hehaka Sapa, or Black Elk, the great Sioux chief, over sixty and nearly blind, reflects upon the invasion, between 1863 and 1890, of his people's lands by the white man, and sadly recounts their treatment of the buffalo. The 'Winter of the Hundred Slain,' to which he refers, is the Fetterman Fight, commonly described as a 'massacre' in which a Captain Fetterman and 81 men were wiped out on Peno Creek near Fort Phil Kearney, December 21, 1866.

'I can remember that winter of the hundred slain (1866) as a man may remember some bad dream he dreamed when he was little, but I can not tell just how much I heard when I was bigger and how much I understood when I was little. It is like some fearful thing in a fog, for it was a time when everything seemed troubled and afraid.

I had never seen a Wasichu [white man] then, and did not know what one looked like; but everyone was saying that the Wasichus were coming and that they were going to take our country and rub us all out and that we should all have to die fighting.

Once we were happy in our own country and we were seldom hungry, for then the two-leggeds and the four-leggeds lived together like relatives, and there was plenty for them and for us. But the Wasichus came, and they have made little islands for us and other little islands for the four-leggeds, and always these islands are becoming smaller, for around them surges the gnawing flood of the Wasichu; and it is dirty with lies and greed.

I was ten years old that winter, and that was the first time I ever saw a Wasichu. At first I thought they all looked sick, and I was afraid they might just begin to fight us any time, but I got used to them.

I can remember when the bison were so many that they could not be counted, but more and more Wasichus came to kill them until there were only heaps of bones scattered where they used to be. The Wasichus did not kill them to eat; they killed them for the metal that makes them crazy, and they took only the hides to sell. Sometimes they did not even take the hides, only the tongues; and I have heard that fire-boats came down the Missouri River loaded with dried bison tongues. You can see that the men who did this were crazy. Sometimes they did not even take the tongues; they just killed and killed because they liked to do that. When we hunted bison, we killed only what we needed.'

(From *Touch the Earth*, 1971, ed. T.C. McLuhan)

And even though humankind *has* gone on to make the attempt to conceptualize more and more of its existence, it is very important for us to note that in still being fundamentally intuitive, every single one of us still has the absolute entirety of our intuitive ability to be *satisfied with enough*. Nonetheless, it would appear that as part of our attempt to conceptualize our experience of existence, we attempted to conceptualize our demand for resources. Thus, our *intuitive demand* was gradually subjugated by a supposedly *conceptualized deman* d for resources.

Given that our intuitive demand for resources is *satisfiable*, it means that this demand is *finite* per unit of time. Therefore, at this level we are dealing with a definable rate of consumption at which a specific quantity of resource consumed will suffice and bring us to a point of contentment, for a certain period of time.

However, at humankind's supposedly conceptualized level of activity, its conceptualized demand for resources is apparently *infinite*. At this level, no matter how much of a given resource you consume, there is *always* the possibility of attemptedly conceptualizing *more* of it; even if, in reality, you have already consumed too much of that resource for your ecological well-being.

Why should this be? Why should an intuitive demand for resources be *finite* per unit of time, and hence be satisfiable, but a supposedly conceptualized demand for resources be *infinite*, and hence eternally unsatisfiable? The reason will become clear, I believe, if we consider carefully what humankind has been trying to do as it has attempted to conceptualize its demand for resources.

Humankind has been attempting to superimpose a supposed, conceptualized demand mechanism on top of its inherent, intuitive demand mechanism. Thus, the attempt is being made to place the 'concept' of 'wanting a given quanitity of resource', over and above the intuitively felt sensation of 'needing a given quantity of resource'. The *experiencable* 'consequence' of this attempt is that a given quantity of resour ce will, in ecological reality, be sought out and consumed, so that at the ecological level, real, intuitive satisfaction will be experienced.

However, it is only to be expected that having tried to create a 'concept' – in this case, of 'wanting a given quantity of resource' – we should also actually want to *experience* the substance of that 'concept' itself. But we can't.

It is not possible for us to actually sense and *experience* the substance of any 'concept', because as we established earlier, 'concepts' don't exist. Since humankind has never been able to conceptualize in an ecologically meaningful way, concepts have never been brought into ecological existence; hence they don't exist, and we can't experience them.

It is at *this* level, of supposed concept-making, that we fail to get any satisfaction. We make the attempt to create concepts but we never succeed in doing so, and our consequent inability to actually, *ecologically* experience them leaves us perpetually dissatisfied. We can never, ever, achieve a 'conceptual satisfaction'.

As an example, the industrialized world (18 per cent of the world's human population) currently produces 70 per cent of the world's traded goods in its attempt to satisfy its conceptualized demand for resources; whilst the rest of the world (82 per cent of the world's population) produces only 30 per cent. Yet in the late twentieth century, the industrialized world is *still* looking for economic *growth* and *higher* levels of production. That is, it is *still* unsatisfied. (Statistics from *Handbook of International Trade and Development Statistics*, 1985 supplement; UNCTAD).

Our supposed, conceptualized wanting
leaves us actually, intuitively wanting,
eternally.

To summarize thus far, what I am saying is that whilst our *intuitive* demand for resources is inherently satisfiable, our supposedly *conceptualized* demand is eternally unsatisfiable, because it involves us in attempting to experience the concepts of our demand for resources, which is ecologically impossible.

Perhaps a more parochial example, which just happens to be to hand, can serve to illustrate the point I am making. On the desk in front of me I have a bag of sultanas to dive into, in my more reflective moments. Whilst I am sitting here, I might feel, intuitively, that I need to eat one. So I eat one and then feel I need another. On consuming the second sultana, however, I feel inside, intuitively, that I have had enough, for the time being at least. My intuitive demand-sensing-mechanism has worked well and has brought me to a point of sultana-satisfaction.

123

Nonetheless, even at this point of intuitively felt satisfaction, I can still supposedly 'think', or attemptedly 'conceptualize' of having some *more* sultanas, and as a consequence I might actually go ahead and consume, shall we say, another thirty sultanas. All the time, underneath, my intuitive-demand sensing-mechanism will be telling me: You've already had enough sultanas... Now you've had enough plus twenty sultanas... Now you've really blown it, and you feel sick. And even at *this* stage, I could still 'think' about consuming *another* thirty sultanas; as is shown by the oft-heard exclamation: 'Just to think of another sultana makes me feel sick!'

However, whilst I have indeed been actually, physically consuming actual, physical sultanas, and whilst I have actually, intuitively been *experiencing* their consumption, I have *not* actually been consuming concepts; it's as if the process of actually *experiencing* frightens away the supposed 'concept' of a thing. But of course the real reason I could not possibly have been consuming the concepts of the sultanas, was because in ecological reality, concepts don't exist – not even 'sultana-concepts'. Consequently, at this level of my attempting to consume and *experience* 'sultana-concepts' there is never any chance of my doing so, and still less of a chance of my ever being able to *experience* a 'conceptual sultana-satisfaction'.

That is, satisfaction at the supposedly conceptual level is not ecologically possible. Thus, my *attempt* to achieve an eternally unattainable conceptual satisfaction has the potential to go on *ad infinitum*, and it is this, our *attempt* to achieve a conceptual satisfaction that is eternally unsatisfiable.

Concepts do not exist. An infinity of effort is the inevitable characteristic of humankind's attempt to experience them.

As Harry Snodgrass Senior once musingly observed:

'Contentment is not a state of 'mind', it's a state of 'being'.'

Two 'infinities' available to us,
of intuitive contentment, the first,
experiencable in our 'here' and 'now';
and we 'here' and 'now' exist.

Of eternal striving, the second,
for a conceptual contentment which,
is supposed to be experiencable 'over there' and 'then';
but where do we exist?
and when?

To conclude this section, I would say that the *intuitive* demand for resources exhibited, for example, by animals, is inherently capable of yielding intuitively-felt satisfaction and contentment. On the other hand, the *conceptualized* demand for resources, as exhibited by an attemptedly conceptualizing, economic humankind, is inherently incapable of yielding intuitively-felt satisfaction and contentment, and thus the expenditure of human effort, in an attempt to attain that satisfaction and contentment, can go on *ad infinitum*. It is, I believe, because of this attempt to achieve conceptual satisfaction that today we all strive after *more* of everything, and seem to be perpetually *accelerating* the rate at which we experience life, because in its being an attemptedly conceptualized economic life, we never manage to experience the contentment which an intuitive living of our lives would allow us.*

Growth – or is it *A* Growth?

Resources are processed by human beings so that they can be used to ensure human survival and contentment. In today's industrialized world, Gross National Product (GNP) statistics are presented annually in almost every country of the world to indicate the quantity of resources processed for this purpose. They are presented either in units of product, tonnages, or in terms of financial value.

Only a relatively small number of official statistics, estimations and computations are ever concerned with the number of units of GNP considered necessary to satisfy the real ecological needs, and hence the demand for resources, of one human adult

---

*And now, after twenty years, I am beginning to understand why I upset my father so much. Working long hours in an attempt to survive in an 'economic' world of eternally unsatisfiable, conceptualized demand; exhorted by a nineteen-year-old son fresh from business college and full of business concepts, my dear father was having to work too hard – and even then I was never satisfied with what he achieved. No wonder he was driven to exclaim: 'I've never done enough'.

for one year. To me, this is indicative of the fact that in most of today's fanatical concern with economic growth, such growth is hardly ever related to human *need*. It is seldom directly related to that which it is meant to nurture; namely, human survival. It is seldom directly related to how many people's survival it is ensuring; nor, importantly, whether the GNP that is being produced is in excess of, or falls short, of a nation's actual human *needs*.

Our interest in GNP and economic growth would therefore seem to have no reference point to make it meaningful in terms of its role in supporting human existence. Apparently, a relationship is *assumed* to exist between GNP and ensuring human survival, and since *increases* in GNP are always sought, the assumed relationship would seem to be that more economic growth supports more human survival.

Consequently, the only thing GNP is ever related to is itself; this year's compared to last year's; this year's compared to the average for the last three years, etc. Such comparisons are usually given in percentage terms, and are referred to as 'economic growth indicators'.

To the extent that anything which exists is a *process*, which means that it will be functioning at a rate, then we can say that plain, straightforward, economic *activity* is a process, and consequently, that it will function at a certain *rate*. In any one year, a certain quantity of resources will go round a given economic system. Therefore, the term economic *growth* is really a label for an increase in the rate at which a given economic system is functioning. An 'increase in rate' can be referred to as *acceleration*, and therefore it would be reasonable for us to say that 'economic growth statistics' are really indicative of the *acceleration in an economic system*.

Now from an ecological point of view, acceleration is all very well, as long as it is periodically tempered with deceleration, to ensure that overall the average rate of a system's functioning remains, shall we say, ecologically containable. A two-dimensional depiction of this phenomenon might look something like this (see overleaf):

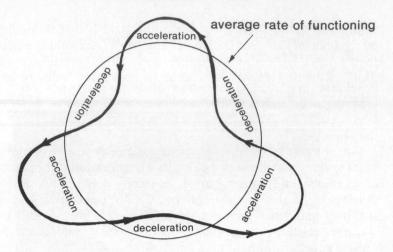

Over short and long periods of time, human functioning displays this sort of characteristic. Sometimes we run, sometimes we walk; sometimes our metabolisms belt away at a tremendous rate, at other times they assume a basal minimum; during our physiological development through childhood and adolescence, there are waves of accelerated development in specific areas of our anatomy, followed by relative quiescence in those areas and an acceleration of development in other areas. The important thing is, however, that overall these bouts of accelerated activity never go beyond the absolute limits of ecological tolerance, nor are they prolonged to the extent that the decelerated resting periods are denied. Thus as we have already mentioned (pp. 112 and 118), in overall terms, and within a given range of variation, there is a broadly optimal rate at which human beings function, whereby their sustainability is optimised.

However, in industrialized countries there is effectively a perpetual insistence on economic growth – that is, on the *acceleration* of economic activity. Therefore the economic exhortation is, in fact, for *perpetual acceleration*. This is not to deny that sometimes an industrialized country's economic growth is negative – that is, there is a deceleration in its economic activity. But when this occurs 'something is wrong', and such a country's economic performance has to be 'put right'. The *real* insistence, the real imperative is that there shall be *continuous acceleration* in a country's economic performance, and we could conjecture such an exhortation might ultimately bring *Homo Economicus* to an escape velocity and propel us out into space:

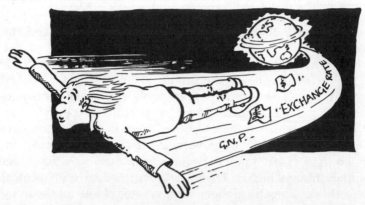

However, in the ecological reality of which we are a part, *perpetual*, and therefore infinite, acceleration cannot exist. As we asserted earlier, even the solar system, within which the Earth is contained, has a rate of turning. And humankind's own rate of functioning meshes in with that solar rate of turning and thereby actually contributes to its stability and to its sustainability. Thus though it is self-regulatory and occurs 'of itself', humankind's rate of functioning relates to and harmonizes with all the other rates of functioning in the solar system and throughout the Universe. It is thus an ecologically 'related' and ecologically 'regulated' rate of functioning. However, continuously accelerating economic growth would seem to be, I believe, part of humankind's overall endeavour to function in an ecologically 'unmoderated' or 'deregulated' way; referring itself only to itself for its rationales, and attempting to shun its inescapable relatedness to ecological rate. And as one comes to such a conclusion, one starts to wonder whether such apparently ecologically deregulated, perpetually accelerating economic growth can be truthfully called 'growth' at all – or whether it is not better described as 'a growth'.

Economic Growth, Investment and Risk

In today's economic world, when a person wishes to acquire resources for her or his survival, she or he will normally find waged or salaried employment, earn some money, and with that money, purchase the resources she or he requires. The risk incurred by the person in following this procedure is relatively low because all the stages in it are well-established and fully recognized.

If, however, the person wishes to get a greater return for his or her endeavour, he or she might go into business. This will normally involve investing a reasonable amount of money into resources and equipment over a protracted period. Thus, although the return at the end of that period might be considerably higher than any wage earned through employment in a similar length of time, the *risk* undertaken will have been commensurately higher. This is because in all such investments, there always lurks the danger that you might lose all the money you have committed to the venture. And where even larger investments are made, larger returns are usually anticipated, but once again, the risks involved will be commensurately higher. In overall terms, what I am saying is that where higher profits are sought, higher risks have to be taken.

Such an equation is not only found in the commercial world. In an ecologically undisturbed environment, seeking higher returns also involves undertaking greater risk. More meat will be made available to a lioness if she kills a fully grown wildebeest as opposed to a fawn, but she undertakes a far greater degree of risk in killing the wildebeest than in killing the fawn; not just because the wildebeest might lash out and injure the lioness, but also because she will have to 'invest' a far greater amount of energy and her chances of success will be much smaller.

There is one factor, however, which I think makes these two types of risk-taking, the commercial and the ecological, qualitatively different. Ecological risk-taking is usually only undertaken up to the level of real ecological *need*, whereas commercial risk-taking knows no limits. This stems from the fact that commercial risk-taking is *conceptualized*, and therefore, as for

130

the conceptualized demand for resources, it has a potential for *infinite* increase, since it can never yield conceptual satisfaction. In terms of conceptualized commercial returns from investment, 'more is better' and therefore there is a propensity towards ever higher risk-taking.

It would seem that in the conceptualized, profit-oriented world of investment and economic growth, we are perpetually being exhorted to take ever-higher risks. However, in the ecological world, getting oneself into higher-risk situations is only undertaken to the extent that it is *necessary*, since in that world 'higher risk' is synonymous with 'reduced safety' and hence with a reduction in the chances for survival.

High Energy Users

As already discussed, satisfaction and contentment can only ever be experienced *intuitively*. Thus if we attempt to achieve contentment by pursuing a conceptualized lifestyle, we will experience only continuing and infinite dissatisfaction, and by increasing our efforts to overcome this, what will inevitability result will be an excessive use of energy. Compared to this, an altogether more intuitive, less highly conceptualized lifestyle offers the possibility of intuitively experienced contentment, since in an intuitive existence, enough is enough. And in such an existence, therefore, energy-use per capita does not need to be so high.

Evidence for this assertion is presented in the book *Ecosystems, energy and population* (1975), by Turk, Witters, Witters and Turk:

> In a natural ecosystem, radiant energy that is received from the sun and trapped in the form of potential energy in plant tissues flows through the food web which consists of various animals and decay organisms, until it is degraded completely into heat and radiated back into space. We showed in Chapter 1 how the system depends upon a continuous inflow of energy from the sun. Moreover, the total amount of sunlight puts a limit on the total metabolism of a system, for the biotic community cannot utilize more energy than it receives. The ecosystems that have existed in the past evolved to survive within these constraints and were very long-lasting.

It is clear that technological man no longer lives within this ancient energy flow pattern. Before the advent of fire, our ancestors needed only 2000 kcals of energy per day per person. The energy used was in the form of food. Later, people domesticated animals, engaged in agriculture, and used fuel for cooking and heating. Per capita energy requirements rose by a factor of roughly six, to 12,000 kcals per day. By 1860, small amounts of coal were being mined, heat engines had been invented, and a resident in London used about 70,000 kcals per day. In Western Europe at this time, the total population and the per capita energy requirements were so high that man needed more energy than could be simultaneously replenished by the sun. He began to use reserves of energy stored as fossils fuels. Such a situation is inherently unstable, for consumption cannot be forever higher than production. In the United States in 1970, man's per capita utilization was 230,000 kcals per day, a rate which greatly accelerates the exhaustion of fossil fuels. This prodigious rate is unique in the history of the world. At no other time, and in no other place, have people utilized energy faster than Americans do today.

The United States, home for six per cent of the population of the world, is responsible for 35 per cent of the world's energy consumption. (See Table 3).

Table 3. Energy Consumption for Selected Nations*

	Per capita daily energy consumption in thousands of kcals	Proportion of world's energy consumption	Proportion of world's population
United States	230	35%	6.0%
Canada	165	3%	0.6%
United Kingdom	145	6%	1.5%
Germany	110	5%	1.5%
USSR	85	16%	7.0%
Japan	40	3%	3.0%
Mexico	30	1%	1.3%
Brazil	15	1%	3.0%
India	6	2%	15.0%

* Data from *Scientific American*, September 1971, p. 142 and *UN Demographic Yearbook*, 1970.

From these statistics we can see that as 'development' and industrialization occur, and hence as the degree of *conceptualized*, ecologically manipulative activity increases in a country, energy-use per capita increases also. In the living of a less ecologically manipulative, less conceptualized lifestyle, which is more accepting of the intrinsic capacities and limitations of humankind's Earthly habitat, there at least exists the possibility of both surviving *and* of achieving contentment which can be derived from intuitively relishing an ecological sufficiency. And quite simply, because such contentment is, in ecological reality, *achievable* by an inherently intuitive humankind, then the living of such a life involves the expenditure of relatively little energy.

It's like,
you're frantically trying to perfect the electric light bulb,
whilst I'm quietly sleeping,
and waiting for the dawn.

***

In highly conceptualized industrialized societies, permeated by the 'more ethic' and the profit-motive, and wracked with the dissatisfaction of never achieving a conceptualized level of contentment, the only diagnosis ever proffered to improve the situation is to put in more and more energy and conceptualized effort. The result is that too much effort is applied to allow such societies to enjoy the sort of contentment that is available, at or about the level of an intuitively-felt, ecologically *adequate* energy input.

As Harry Snodgrass wryly commented in 1911:

'Too much' is not 'enough'.

When, however, humankind functions at a level of energy-input which *is* adequate to ensure its ecological survival and psychological wellbeing, then as an ecological component of an ecologically-paced reality, it will display an ecologically optimal energy efficiency. (For further discussion on this topic, see

133

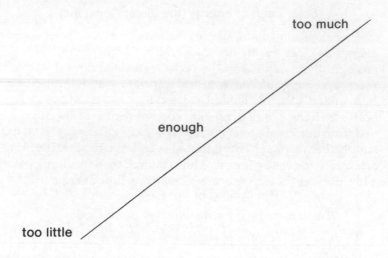

Ecology, 1975, by E.P. Odum, pp. 64 – 67.) Any serious devia-
tion from this ecologically optimal rate of functioning will
inevitably show itself in a relatively inefficient use of energy.

And this, I believe, is precisely what has manifested itself, as
an attemptedly conceptualizing, ecologically manipulative,
economic humankind has tried harder and harder to achieve an
eternally denied conceptual contentment. It has gone past the
point of an ecologically *optimal* rate of functioning, and hence
beyond a point of optimal energy efficiency, with the consequence that its activities have now become energy-inefficient.

To substantiate this assertion let us first of all put the topic
of energy efficiencies into perspective by looking at the entirety
of our Earth's ecosystem; and then, as an example, let us
consider the change in energy efficiencies that has occurred, as
humankind's agricultural techniques have become more and
more conceptualized and energy-intensive.

The main source of energy for the cycling of the Earth's
ecosystem is the Sun, and an amount of energy, referred to as
the 'solar constant' (see *Ecology*, 1975, by E.P. Odum), enters
our ecosystem and causes it to cycle at a globally optimized,
ecological rate. Thus there has evolved, over 4–5 billion years,

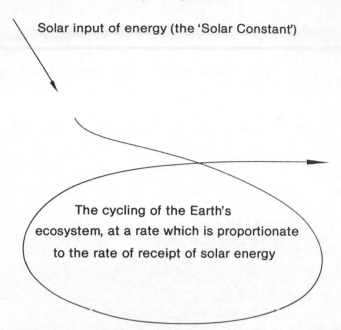

Solar input of energy (the 'Solar Constant')

The cycling of the Earth's
ecosystem, at a rate which is proportionate
to the rate of receipt of solar energy

an 'ecological proportionality' between the rate of receipt of energy from the Sun, and the rate at which the Earth's ecosystem cycles.

When functioning at or about its ecologically proportionate rate, the Earth's ecosystem displays what we might call an 'ecological, evolutionary energy efficiency'. However as we said earlier, where 'separated-out' or 'distilled-off' energy is injected into the components of the Earth's ecosystems which are being used by industrialized humankind, boosting their rate of cycling and hence their productivity, then such accelerated ecosystems begin to lose their ecological rate proportionality and consequently they start to exhibit worsening energy efficiencies. From an ecological point of view they start to become relatively energy-inefficient.

We can get an indication of this phenomenon in data which relate to humankind's long-term agricultural and food-procuring activities. In Chapter 24 of *Agricultural Ecology* (1979), Cox and Atkins show that less highly accelerated agricultural sys-

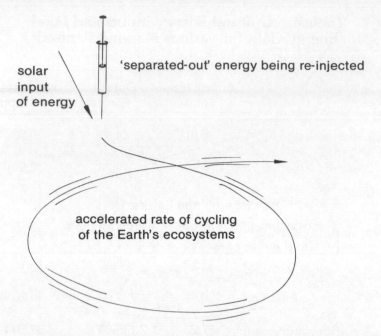

solar
input
of energy

'separated-out' energy being re-injected

accelerated rate of cycling
of the Earth's ecosystems

tems, such as pastoralism, shifting-cultivations and flood irriga-
tion agricultures, yield more energy in the form of food than
the total amount of energy invested in them; whilst today's
energy-intensive, highly accelerated agricultural systems yield
less energy in the form of food than the amounts of energy
invested in them.

If we look at Table 4 opposite (taken from *Agricultural
Ecology*) we can see that the pastoralist, shifting-cultivation and
flood-irrigation systems produce at least 9 times more food
energy than the energy invested in them, and that most permanent agricultures achieve output-over-input ratios between 3
and 1. If however we now consider a modern agricultural
system, such as that currently practised in the United States
(Table 5), we find that the relationship between the energy put
into food production and the energy thereby generated is
reversed. In overall terms in the United States *more energy is
put into agricultural food production than that which is gained
from it.*

Table 4. Cultural Energy Inputs and Food Energy Gain for various Non-mechanised Agricultural Systems

System	Cultural input Total	Output Food	Food output / Total input
1. pastoralist Africa	0.51	4.95	9.70
2. semipastoralist Uganda	6.90	19.70	2.90
3. shifting cultivation New Guinea	139.00	2,278.00	16.40
4. shifting cultivation Thailand	34.60	622.00	18.00
5. shifting cutlivation Mexico	67.57	684.30	10.10
6. shifting cutlivation Sudan	20.98	297.00	14.20
7. shifting cutlivation Zaire	57.27	2,145.00	37.50
8. flood irrigation Thailand	15.20	573.00	37.70
9. paddy irrigation Thailand	41.40	940.00	22.70
10. permanent farming Mexico	97.94+	331.23	3.38
11. permanent farming India	283.76+	270.93	0.95
12. permanent farming Philippines	183.13+	600.40	0.95
13. permanent farming Nigeria	272.22+	247.17	0.91

+ totals include calorific value of seeds and other miscellaneous inputs.

Table 5. Approximate Energy Budget
United States Agriculture in 1970
(based on several sources)

Cultural energy inputs:

Irrigation	133 x 10^{12} kcal
Fertilizers	150 x 10^{12} kcal
Pesticides	12 x 10^{12} kcal
Fuel (other than for irrigation)	326 x 10^{12} kcal
Machinery	101 x 10^{12} kcal
Electricity	107 x 10^{12} kcal
Total cultural energy input	**829 x 10^{12} kcal**

Food energy output

Consumption (200 x 10^6 people at 1.095 x 10^6 kcal/ind/yr)	219 x 10^{12} kcal
Wastage of produced food (20% of above)	24 x 10^{12} kcal
Grain export (40 x 10^6 tons at 4 x 10^6 kcal/ton)	160 x 10^{12} kcal
Total food energy output	**403 x 10^{12} kcal**

Ratios:

Food consumed Input/output	3.08
Food exported Input/output	0.50
Food production Input/output	**2.06**

From Agricultural Ecology by G. W. Cox and M. D. Atkins,
© 1979 by W. H. Freeman & Co. Used by permission.

The essence of agriculture is the application of cultural energy in order to direct biological production into channels where it can be utilized more easily by man. The greater the modification of natural processes that man attempts in this process, the greater is the energy cost he must bear. Non-mechanized systems of pastoralism and shifting cultivation use cultural energy in the form of human labour and realize returns that vary from 5 to nearly 40 calories of food energy per calorie of cultural energy invested. Permanent farming systems in which draft animals are used increase the cultural energy investment, yet still retain a very high efficiency in relation to the investment of industrial or fossil fuel energy.

In mechanized farming, however, industrial energy is invested in large quantities, enabling high levels of production to be achieved with minimum investments of human labour. For most grains, such as corn, wheat and rice, these systems obtain only 1 to 3 calories of food energy per calorie of cultural energy. For many fruits and vegetables, and for all forms of animal protein, the return is less than the investment. The energy costs of protein production vary greatly, however. Plant proteins in grains can be produced for about 3 to 5 calories per calorie of protein; concentrated plant protein analogues of meat for 10 to 20 calories; and milk, pork, and feedlot beef for 30 to 80 calories.'

(from Agricultural Ecology, 1979
by Cox and Atkins, Chapter 24)

Obviously, the less accelerated systems referred to in this comparison are not completely ecologically *non*-manipulative. Pastoralist systems, shifting-cultivation and flood-irrigation systems etc. are clearly 'conceptualized' systems of food procurement, and result from the human attempt to lead a conceptualized existence. But such relatively ancient systems do, to a reasonable degree, harmonize with, and are accepting of, the ecological parameters and characteristics of the environments within which they exist. They demonstrate food production energy efficiencies which are at least *nearer* to the evolutionary ecological energy efficiencies of ecosystems which have not been extensively disrupted by highly conceptualized agricultural manipulation.

This comparison substantiates the overall assertion that there has been a general trend towards greater energy *inefficiency*, as we have 'progressed' from less-conceptualized, to more highly conceptualized systems of human activity.

This must be the case, I believe, because in organizing and maintaining today's economic, conceptualized, energy-intensive systems of activity (that is, systems injected with ecologically excessive amounts of distilled-off energy), humankind is attempting to instill relative *imbalance* into a dynamically self-balancing reality, *acceleration* into a paced reality, and *dislocation* into a cohesive reality.

All such conceptualized activity is part of the attempt by a conceptualizing humankind to function in a way which is at odds with the very qualities of the ecological systems on which it relies, and of which it is a part. It's little wonder that such activities ultimately prove to be energy-inefficient – quite apart from the fact that they still can't afford us any conceptualized contentment.

Energy is the first pollutant

Another result of the perpetual increase in our use of energy-intensive techniques and technologies is that we are now 'polluting' our Earth's ecosystems with *energy*. According to conceptualized whim, we take energy from one part of our global ecosystem and inject it into another part, and expect that our conceptualized management of that injected energy will cause those ecosystems to function in an ecologically balanced, ecologically paced and ecologically sustainable way – just as they did before. We also think that the conceptualized management of those ecosystems will be every bit as ecologically optimal as when ecosystems optimized their own functioning 'of themselves'. We assume that the manipulative injection of such separated-out energy will yield nothing but benefits to humankind, and that there will be no concomitant ecological bill to pay in the short- or long-term.

However in reality the result of such actions is that the *ecological integrity* of the ecosystems that are thus injected is first of all strained and subsequently ruptured. 'Pollution' is the exudate from such enforced ecological rupturing, and it is the injection of separated-out, ecologically excessive amounts of energy that is causing it.

Our global ecosystem not only *generates* resources, it also *dissembles* and re-assimilates them as well, so that they are available for re-use in subsequent millennia. In the glory of our ecosystem's self-regulatory capability, generation and reassimilation mesh with one another to create a self-balancing cycle of events. On further consideration we can see that this cycle of events has both qualitative and quantitative aspects.

Qualitatively, the resources which the world's ecosystems produce have to be of a type which can also be broken down and re-assimilated into that system. That is, they have to be *qualitatively* compatible with the world's systems of generation and re-assimilation. Thus if we consider, for example, the Earth's biotic production, we find that the ecological quality of the vegetative and animal materials generated is such that they can be broken down and can re-enter the Earth's mineral reserves, ready for re-assimilation in later biotic productivity. Calcium, for example, that once formed the shells of small shell fish, is deposited on the sea-bed and is gradually compressed by subsequent layers of sediment to form limestone. Over geological time, such limestone might end up forming the foundation of a land-based agricultural area, from which human beings satisfy their own needs for calcium via the plants in the field and the milk from the cows that feed upon them.

In quantitative terms the world's ecosystem has to generate *amounts* of produce which it is capable of re-assimilating in a given unit of time. That is, the global ecosystem's rate of resource production has to be compatible with its rate of resource re-assimilation. As an example, consider the cycling of nitrogen in the soil of an uncultivated area of land. The quantity of available nitrogen in the soil facilitates a *certain quantity* of primary and subsequent biotic production, which the detritus food-chain is then capable of breaking down. In this way, a similar quantity of nitrogen is returned to the soil for mixing with newly released nitrogen, ready for subsequent re-generation into new biotic

141

material. (See *Agricultural Ecology* by Cox and Atkins, 1979, pp. 318-19, figure 12-17.)

However, in wanting *more* resources from the Earth's ecosystems than would otherwise be available, a conceptualizing, ecologically manipulative humankind pumps ecologically excessive amounts of energy into those ecosystems. Qualitatively, the result of such energy-intensive manipulation is that substances can now be produced which are no longer ecologically compatible, in terms of type, with our ecosystem's processes of generation and re-assimilation. For example, if we consider humankind's relationship with pest insects as an ecosystem in its own right, then we would find that in previous, *low-energy-input* agricultural systems, insects did indeed damage certain percentages of the crops being grown, but indigenous natural predators that had evolved along with the 'pests' moderated the extent of their impact. In the late twentieth century, however, an *energy-intensive* agro-chemical industry has provided us with, for example, the chlorinated hydrocarbons which do the same job but which, after they have been used, cannot be broken down by our ecosystem's natural cycles of ecological decay (See *Silent Spring* by Rachel Carson, 1962). They therefore persist in the Earth's ecosystem, as what we might call 'qualitative pollutants'; the polluting result of humankind's *initial injection of ecologically excessive energy* into the 'humankind – pest insect' ecosystem.

In quantitative terms, the energy-intensive manipulation of the Earth's ecosystem means that whilst humankind does indeed make more *resources* available for its consumption, in the short-term a concomitant increase in the quantity of *resource-residues* also occurs, and this augmented level of residues can prove more than the ecosystem can naturally break down and re-assimilate in a given unit of time. As a result of humankind's *energy-intensive* acceleration of some of the Earth's ecosystems, the rate of residue production outstrips the rate of residue re-assimilation.

We could reasonably label this 'quantitative pollution', and an important example of this type of pollution can be seen in the energy-intensive development of human transportation systems. In walking and running, humankind exhales CO_2, but in quantities which can be assimilated by the Earth's vegetation. However, in our current use of the internal combustion engine, on the land, in the oceans and in the sky, we have vastly increased the quantity of the CO_2 exhausts we produce, just to move ourselves around. As a result, and together with the simultaneous decimation of the tropical rain forests, which are significant absorbers of CO_2, we are now 'quantitatively polluting' our global atmosphere with CO_2, thereby increasing its capacity to retain incoming solar radiation and contributing to the 'greenhouse effect'.

Now, whilst most people would agree that such 'quantitative' and 'qualitative' types of pollution are undesirable and unacceptable, what has to be said in addition to this is that, at a more fundamental level, and underpinning both these forms of pollution, there exists what we might call the 'primary polluting effect' of humankind's injection of *ecologically excessive amounts of energy* into the ecosystems on which we rely for our survival. For it is these injections of extra energy that damage the *functional integrity* of the ecosystems in the first place.

Quantitative and qualitative pollution are merely the subsequent manifestations of the primary polluting effect of humankind's injection of ecologically excessive amounts of energy into the Earth's ecosystems.

'Would you pass me the sugar, please?'

Inflation – or is it 'inflammation'?

In lay terms 'inflation' means paying more money than before for the same thing. In a monetarized economy, where you can't get anything unless you pay for it, this means that the thing you want has become harder to get.

Why should this occur? I think the answer is that on a global scale the industrial base of our monetarized economies has accelerated the rate at which it is taking resources from the Earth's ecosystem, to the extent that the Earth's ecosystem can no longer furnish the supply as easily or as consistently as it could before.

For example, if the maximum sustainable harvest from a herring stock is x tons each year and you take $x + 1000$ tons, that inherent sustainablility is undermined. The stock will become progressively more depleted, there will be fewer herring caught, and their price will be inflated. The industrial base of our monetarized economies has been consistently accelerating the rate at which it is taking resources from the Earth's ecosystem because it has had to comply, and continues to have to comply, with the imperative of achieving economic growth. That is, its resource-use has had to *accelerate* to allow it to 'grow' economically. However, as we have said before, over time, the functioning of the Earth's ecosystem occurs at a variable, though broadly consistent, *rate*. Therefore, to be sustainable, humankind's off-take of resources must similarly occur at a broadly consistent *rate*, and one which is *within*, and hence can be accommodated by, the ecological rate of functioning of the ecosystem. But as we have just said, it does not.

Humankind's off-take of resources from the Earth's ecosystem has been occurring at an accelerating rate ever since a newly conceptualizing humankind began to manipulate its environment, and in particular, since it instigated the processes of mechanization and industrialization. Thus today the industrial base of our economies is taking resources at a highly *accelerated rate*, from an ecosystem which still functions, and which can only function, at *a broadly consistent ecological rate*.

The differential between these two rates sets up a *friction* and I believe that this friction finds its monetary manifestation in inflation – or is it 'inflammation'?

Unemployment

The mechanized injection of ecologically excessive amounts of energy into the processing of resources for human consumption has also been the cause of human 'unemployment'.

Mechanization and, more recently, computerization have provided the gadgets whereby a conceptualizing and environmentally manipulative humankind has injected ecologically excessive amounts of distilled-off energy into the functioning of the ecosystems on which it relies for survival. Where previously human energy and skill was being fully applied to ensure the procurement and processing of resources, now its expenditure has been rendered partially superfluous because conceptualized, mechanized and computerized energy and skill have been employed to do most of the work instead.

This has occurred because the use of mechanized energy, and more recently computerized energy, has quickly shown itself to be 'cheaper' than the use of human energy. In the first place, this is because of the current plentitude of fossil-fuel reserves, and secondly because of humankind's increased ingenuity in harnessing those reserves for its own purposes.

Underpinning all this, however, is the fact that by the time mechanized energy was being conceptualized and brought into being, the economic, or rather the 'financial' evaluation of phenomena was already a well-established procedure. Therefore, as mechanized energy became available, it was subjected, not to ecologically meaningful 'resource-evaluation' – in which the energy value of what comes *out of* mechanized processes is compared to the energy being pumped *into* them – but rather to financial evaluation which, because of fossil-based energy's increasing availability, showed it to be 'cheaper'.

Had resource-evaluation been applied to the use of fossil-based energy, it would have shown that the machine-intensive procedures which were evolving (such as the energy-intensive agricultural systems, considered on pages 136–140) were increasingly energy-inefficient. Resource-evaluation would have shown that, in terms of resources, the use of mechanized and subsequently computerized energy is 'dearer'.

Thus, it is because the assessment of mechanized and computerized energy has been made in financial rather than resource-use terms that our monetarized societies have adopted mechanized and computerized systems on a worldwide basis. The application of human energy to the procurement of resources for our survival has consequently been substituted by mechanized and computerized energy, and 'human unemployment' has arisen as a direct result.

With the occurrence of this human unemployment, a seventh level can be added to the six levels of ecological dislocation already being experienced by a significant proportion of humankind, referred to earlier on pp 103–104:

> *Seventh level:* such employees being made 'unemployed' as mechanized and computerized energy has been substituted for human energy and skill, because it is financially 'cheaper'.

Today, millions of resourceless people in both the developed and the developing worlds have been condemned to a state of unemployment. And whereas in the time before the use of mechanical and computerized energy, it was at least necessary to *involve* resourceless people, via employment, in the processing of life-essential resources, now not only are resourceless people effectively 'dislocated' from their resource-base, they are also being denied any effective involvement in the processing of the resources they need for survival.

This state of affairs has been brought about principally, I believe, by the mechanized and computerized injection of ecologically excessive amounts of energy into the ecosystems on which we rely for our survival.

Industrialization

In essence, industrialization represents the accelerated processing of resources demanded by economic societies. In order to achieve this acceleration, industrialized countries have injected large amounts of additional energy into their systems of resource-processing. This is illustrated, as mentioned earlier, by the much higher per capita use of energy in industrialized countries, compared to non-industrialized countries. Table 6 (see overleaf) gives another example of this astounding discrepancy in energy-use, which was recently presented in the World Commission on Environment and Development's report, *Our Common Future* (1987).

In energy-intensive industrialized countries, not only has this process of industrialization manifested itself in an excessively high use of energy, but it has also been the means of consolidating, and indeed exacerbating, the effective *separation* of many of the world's populations from their countries' resource base. Industrialization has brought this about by 'extending' the chain of processing of resources, and as with the acceleration of that chain of processing, its extension has only been made possible by the injection of extra energy. As a result, in the industrialized world, we now have very long systems of resource-processing. For example, the pen with which I am writing was purchased in

147

Table 6. Global Primary Energy Consumption Per Capita, 1984

World Bank GNP Economy Category	GNP per capita (1984 $)	Energy consumption (kw per capita*)	Mid–1984 population (million)	Total consumption (TW)
Low Income	260	0.41	2,390	0.99
Sub-Saharan Africa	210	0.08	258	0.02
Middle Income	1,250	1.07	1,188	1.27
Lower-middle	740	0.57	691	0.39
Upper-middle	1,950	1.76	497	0.87
Sub-Saharan Africa	680	0.25	148	0.04
High-Income Oil Exporters	11,250	5.17	19	0.10
Industrial Market Economies	11,430	7.01	733	5.14
East European Non-Market Economies	–	6.27	389	2.44
World	–	2.11**	4,718	9.94

* Kw per capita is kW years/year per capita.

** Population-weighted average energy consumption (kW/capita) for first three main categories is 0.654 and for industrial market and East European categories is 6.76.

Source: Based on World Bank, *World Development Report 1986*, New York, Oxford University Press, 1986

England, having been made in America from plastics derived from oil which probably came from the Middle East; the rice I ate for lunch was purchased in a local shop, having been purchased from an importer-wholesaler, who had imported it from America, where it had been grown, perhaps using fertilizers from another country, etc.

Whereas initially the human being who dealt with a raw material from his or her local environment quite probably consumed or used the product that resulted, now that same resource might pass from:

resource owner
to primary processor
to a secondary processor
to a component manufacturer
to an assembler
to an importer
to a wholesaler
to a retailer and finally, to a consumer.

This extension in resource-processing has resulted, I believe, because down the centuries, commercial and industrial entrepreneurs have perceived profitable extensions in the line of resource-processing. From an ecological point of view, however, this development can be seen to have been instrumental in further *separating* the consuming majority of humankind from the resource-base of which it is a part.

Specialization

The extension in the chain of resource-processing has, over the centuries, nurtured the evolution of 'specialists' who contribute their specialized skills at various stages in the extending chain. Whereas in a less highly conceptualizing, less ecologically manipulative, less industrialized society each person might well have been conversant with a range of skills and activities on which their survival depended, in an industrialized situation this is no longer the case. Here, the development of specialized processes means in effect that most people are *not* conversant with the majority of the processes on which, at the end of the day, they rely for survival.

In a less ecologically manipulative society most people in a community would have had a very wide range of knowledge and skills, each of which would have been critically important in ensuring survival: the ability to find and tap water sources;

knowledge of plant species and their uses; house-building; hunting; clothes-making and tool-making, etc. However, when communities began converting from a nomadic lifestyle to a more settled existence, the opportunity for specialized activity increased greatly.

For one thing, this shift resulted in a reduction in the range of environments encountered. Instead of an awareness of, for example, highland climates in the summer and lowland climates in the winter, human beings who had settled permanently on a lowland plain would now only have to cope with a lowland climate – in both winter and summer. There was a *narrowing* and *deepening* of experience.

This is not to say that throughout the other millions of years of their evolution *Homo erectus* and *Homo sapiens* have not had skills and capabilities which have been changing in both breadth and depth: they have, continually. All that I am saying here is that at this particular juncture in our development, when our lifestyle evolved into a more conceptualized form of existence, the specific change which occurred was a narrowing and a deepening of our experiences and activity. Thus I believe we can reasonably say that at about this time human activities and skills changed from a 'generalized form' into a more specific or 'specialized' form.

In addition, on changing to a more highly conceptualized form of existence, human activity changed in character from being *accepting and satisfied with* what the environment offered, to activity which involved *intervention* and the forceful increase of an environment's yield capability. In a less conceptualized lifestyle there is a grateful acceptance of that which a given series of environments provides – a nomadic lifestyle is accepting of natural yields and is accepting of the need to move in harmony with the varying seasons of fruitfulness. Indeed, nomadism is a perpetual expression of faith in the environment and in the seasons of the year. On the other hand, a more settled lifestyle necessitates a greater degree of environmental intervention. It involves going across a boundary, from 'satisfaction' and 'acceptance', to 'dissatisfaction' and 'intervention'. And in going across this boundary something very significant occurs.

In assuming the *authority* to intervene and intentionally augment an environment's supply systems, humankind also assumed the concomitant *responsibility* of ensuring the continued, successful functioning of those systems. This, I believe, was a truism which was unperceived at the time, and which though now recognized has continued to be ignored up to the present day. The essential thing that has to be said about this change is that the move to intervene brought with it an *intensification* in the nature of humankind's relationship with its environment. From being satisfied and grateful, humankind became dissatisfied and interventionist, and in so becoming, it took on an environmental responsibility which *intensified* the tenor of its relationship with its environment.

Thus, over thousands of years, there occurred a *narrowing*, a *deepening* and an *intensification* in humankind's relationship with its environment, and these formed the beginnings of the process we now know as 'specialization'. It is only by thus considering the extremely long periods of time over which the specialization of human skills has occurred that we can in any way explain the extent to which it has evolved. Today, the phenomenon we know as 'specialization' is global in its spread and extreme in the degree of its development. The supply of water, the supply of energy, transportation, medical care, the production of food, etc. – all our basic requirements now involve the use of specialized skills and technologies.

This in itself is not too uncomfortable, until we begin to realize the extent to which this state of affairs *separates* and distances the average man and woman from the knowledge, skills and expertise on which his/her survival depends. If we consider the production of food, for example, we find that many people in the 'developed' world have little idea as to how their food is produced or processed; if we consider the supply of water, very few people today know where their water comes from, nor how it is treated to make it drinkable.

The average man or woman is ignorant about these processes because they have become 'specializations', understood only by their respective specialists. This *separation* from the specialist

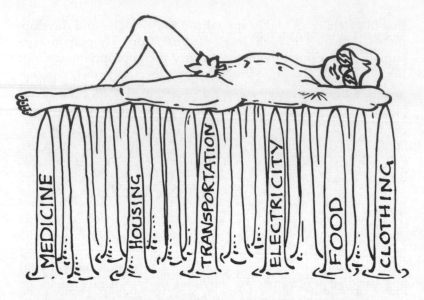

As a society, we live on the pinnacles of our specializations.

knowledge on which our basic needs are provided is, I would contend, a worrying phenomenon.

With regard to a human being's continued survival, it is bad enough when he/she is ignorant as to the means whereby *just one* life-essential is provided, but the fact of the matter is that most people today are ignorant of *most* of the specialisms which provide their basic needs. This is because most people today are themselves specialists in one field or another. They will have had to become specialists to maximize their own economic viability, and in so becoming, they will have had little time or opportunity to have become conversant with the remaining specializations on which they rely for survival.

Another result of specialization is that specialists can only be asked meaningful questions by people who are themselves thoroughly conversant with that given specialism. This means that the yield from highly specialized technologies and developments demands a high level of *trust* from lay-person consumers, who cannot themselves verify the appropriateness, nor the quality, of specialist-produced articles. Conversely specialists have to accept what must appear to them to be a profound lack of appreciation with regard to the fruits of their specialized endeavours, from lay-people who, for no fault of their own, have no idea as to how much effort has gone into the development and production of a 'new' specialist product. There is thus an 'appreciation gap' between specialists and lay-people.

In overall terms, the reason for pointing out the extent to which we are all dependent on specialist knowledge, predominantly ignorant about that specialist knowledge, and at one side or another of an 'appreciation gap', is that this results in a tremendous *separation* and divide in our lives. For if we are predominantly ignorant about the knowledge whereby all our basic requirements are provided, how can any of us be involved with the decisions that have to be made on the use of such specialist knowledge, or indeed on the direction of its further development?

***

I think it is reasonable to say that humankind's loss of its 'ecological sensibility' results, to some degree, from the specialization of human knowledge. This is because the process of specialization involves not only the creation of a dividing line between the knowledge held by specialists and that held by the majority of lay-people, but it also creates a dividing line between specialisms, cutting-up the entirety of human knowledge into separate categories. As a result, not only is it difficult for the specialist to talk to the lay-person, but it is also difficult for one specialist to talk to another, about inter-specialist relationships.

The result is that in the twentieth century the entirety of human knowledge is strongly compartmentalized – yet *another* example of the fundamental 'assumption of separability', that can be found seeping through and oozing out of all conceptualized human endeavour.

Communications that Keep us Apart

One of the industrialized world's current specializations is its high-tech 'communications' industry. Most British people can travel the length and breadth of the UK efficiently and swiftly by road and rail; can pick up a telephone and speak to someone in America, or fly there by plane; and can sit in their homes and watch something 'live' on the television, that is perhaps happening on the other side of the world.

Such 'communications' do indeed facilitate communication, but at considerable cost; not, that is, financial cost, but rather in terms of human-scale relating and communing. Thus whereas before, for example, some of the members of a family, at home in the evening, might have talked to one another, maybe sung a song or done something together; now television allows them to sit in the same room and not have to relate to one another. The result is that in human terms, the room is silent, though technologically, it is noisy. A television in a room is a 'plug-hole' into which people's 'being' and attention is poured.

On a larger scale, and thanks to the developments in long-distance communication technologies such as our road, rail, air and sea links, our fixed physical environment – our homes, colleges, and factories etc. – have spread themselves out over increasingly large distances. Thus whereas previously, people of one grouping or family tended to live, work and play in one community, locality or area, today families are increasingly strewn over all parts of a country, or even continent, strung together only by these energy-intensive, modern communication systems. Once again, this requires disruption of human-scale communication.

Previously, indigenous production and craft workshops were predominantly localized and served local markets, but today, a multi-national company's factories can be thousands of miles apart and their market can be global. Yet their whole operation will be co-ordinated by energy-intensive, world-shrinking communication systems and the employees of such multi-national companies concern themselves daily with problems, deals and situations 'elsewhere'.

At all these levels, high-energy, high-tech communication systems are increasingly facilitating technological communication with a 'somewhere-else', which is creating an effective *separation* from the 'here' in which people's real ecological lives occur.

Consumerism, the 'Throw-away' Society and Vandalism

When mechanized and computerized energy has effectively separated most people from putting their own effort into the procurement of essential resources, and when specialist knowledge has precluded them from a knowledge of 'how' those essential resources are produced, all that is left is to 'consume'. The resultant 'consumers' are so *distanced* from what goes into the manufacture of consumer items, that there is little reverence for them. In turn, this provides the appropriate psychological seedbed in which to nurture the concept of the 'throw-away' society.

Simultaneously, the growing disrespect for material things finds a more extreme expression in 'vandalism' But in terms of resource-use what exactly is the difference between vandalism and a throw-away society? Which is the more irreverent? Kicking a telephone kiosk to pieces, or throwing away millions of tons of re-usable paper, steel, glass and wood, and billions of plastic bottles and containers that are still functionally perfect? *Both* are symptomatic of an irreverence for resources which is borne of our consumer society's effective *separation* from its resource-base, and of its effective *separation* from any meaningful involvement in the procurement of the resources that are essential for its survival.

And This Is How It Works ... (a resumé)

Up to this point in our deliberations we have considered some of the concepts which go to make up at least part of the basis of our current economic system. And whilst several of these concepts do indeed attempt to be divisive, as we have just seen, for example, with specialization and communications, nonetheless the system as a whole has evolved into a *cohesive* functioning entity. This is because today's economic system is a *consequence* of humankind's attempt to create a conceptualized existence for itself, and as such it actually 'exists', and is part of an ecologically cohesive reality.

The section which follows is an attempt to highlight this fact. Because it is a summary of all that has gone before, this section may seem repetitive, but it is included in the hope that the *cohesive* and hence self-reinforcing nature of our economic system's complementary components is made clear.

One of the consequences of humankind's attempt to create a conceptualized lifestyle for itself was its ecologically manipulative employment of its own capabilities and those of the ecosystems on which it relied for survival. This was in order that it could get *more* resources for its own consumption from those ecosystems than had been the case in 'pre-conceptualizing' times. The long-term ecological result of this was that ecologically maintainable rates of resource-supply were eventually exceeded, and the sustainability of the ecosystems thus exploited began to decline.

However in the short term this conceptualized human manipulation of the environment did yield more resources than in 'pre-conceptualizing' times, and it thereby facilitated an increase in the size of the human population. The new areas which were consequently colonized by ecologically exploitative populations inevitably contained ecologically harmonious groups of human beings, however, and the human:human conflict which followed thus only occurred *after* human:habitat conflict and exploitation had already been instigated. This in turn put greater demands on the environments in which humankind was living, and whilst the colonization of new habitats increased, so too did the intensity with which human effort was applied to already-settled areas.

Human, conceptualized agricultural settlement resulted, and in turn this gradually transformed what had previously been the human sense of 'belonging to' an area or habitat, into a belief that the area 'belonged to' the human beings who were now putting so much conceptualized effort into its functioning. However, the subsequent acknowledgement of the 'ownership' of resources necessitated an acceptance of the premise that the 'owned' resource was permanently unavailable to, and hence effectively 'separated from', all people other than its owner. Despite this premise being meaningless in an ecologically cohesive reality, the concept of ownership gradually took root.

Human beings are intuitively capable of experiencing states of physical and psychological contentment; they are capable of sensing when they have had 'enough' of a given thing. This is just one manifestation of the ecological fact that a thing cannot 'be' more than it 'is'. But supposed concepts know no such states of sufficiency nor of contentment, and the concept of ownership was no exception to this rule. Once established, therefore, the effort to own resources proved insatiable. As soon as human beings began to own resources they perceived the power in it, and sought to own more, and in this way, the concept of greed took root. Previously, resources had been used and consumed by human beings to satisfy their ecological *needs*, and thus a community would cooperate to ensure a free flow of resources to all members according to those needs. But once ownership had created barriers to that free flow of resources, the 'exchanging' of resources became necessary; and where previously the free flow of resources had resulted in an even and balanced distribution in the *chances for survival* for members of a community, the even and balanced *exchange of resources* resulted in human beings only receiving according to what they already had. That is, people began to receive resources according to the amount of exchange-power they had, and this was based on the amount of resources they already owned.

Resource-rich owners now, therefore, perceived their resource-poor colleagues to be in a relatively weak bargaining position and began to impose upon them unbalanced demands for resources in any exchanges that occurred. Thus, resource-rich owners began to take *more* resources than they gave. The conceptualization of 'profit' institutionalised the practice of unbalanced exchange, so that the exchange of resources only took place if the resource-rich owner stood to take more resources than he or she gave in return.

In 'pre-ownership' times, all members of any human community would have been variously 'busy' obtaining and processing the resources they needed for survival. However, the human beings who by now had had all their resources 'owned away' from them through unbalanced exchanges, and who were therefore *resourceless*, no longer had any resources on which to be busy. Effectively, they had been made 'employable'. On the other hand, resource-rich owners were now in need of extra energy with which to work and process their excessive holdings of resources. The conceptualization and institutionalizsation of the 'employment' of resourceless human beings was thus logically arrived at.

The global imbalance in the distribution of owned resources not only resulted in the evolution of the concept of employment, however, it also caused our current global population explosion. This is because the imbalance in the distribution of resources gives a minority of the human population more than sufficient social and material means to stabilize the increase in their numbers. The majority, however, who are experiencing a concomitant and ecologically inevitable shortage in material means, are left in an 'in-between-state' of socio-economic development, in which their population increase becomes explosive.

Whilst humankind's attempt to conceptualize had resulted in the social consequences outlined above, it had also resulted in the supposed evolution of a highly analytical human 'mind'. Scientific and technological experimentation was employed to confirm conceptualized hypotheses. Amongst other things, this resulted in the creation of technologies which enabled humankind to avail itself of 'separated-out' amounts of supplementary *energy*.

The industrial application of mechanized and computerized energy has facilitated a massive acceleration in the processing of resources for human utilization; but even this has not been able to satisfy our modern economic societies' ever-accelerating demand for processed goods. This conceptualized demand is inherently unsatisfiable because conceptualized satisfaction and contentment are eternally unattainable. Satisfaction and contentment are only ever intuitively felt.

Nonetheless, in pursuing perpetual economic acceleration, generally referred to as 'economic growth', industrialized societies have continued to attempt to satisfy this eternally unsatisfiable conceptualized demand. In so doing, they have had to inject ecologically excessive amounts of supplementary energy into the Earth's ecosystems. The energy efficiencies of the energy-intensive systems that have resulted have declined proportionately, so that *energy* itself has now become the primary pollutant of the ecosystems on which humankind relies for its survival.

In the meantime, at the interface between our consumer societies' industrial base and the Earth's pool of resources, a discrepancy has evolved between the broadly consistent rate at which our Earth can supply us with essential resources in the long term, and the forever-accelerating rate at which humankind proceeds to use them. The *friction* created by the discrepancy in these rates find its monetary manifestation in 'inflation'.

Recently, the more extensive use of mechanized and computerized energy has been 'cheaper' than the use of human energy because it is currently plentiful. But it is only cheaper when evaluated in financial terms. When evaluated in ecological terms, and specifically in terms of energy efficiencies, then it is seen to be 'dearer'. However, since we currently live in a monetarized economic system this fact is ignored, and as a result the use of much human labour has been dubbed 'economically unviable' – and human unemployment has resulted.

Thus human 'employment', which previously acted as an anaesthetic to mitigate the hurt of an enforced state of resourcelessness for tens of millions of people in the industrialized world, is being withdrawn, and the full force of their actual state of resourcelessness is beginning to hurt once again.

The industrial application of mechanized and computerized energy has also facilitated the global spread of an extended chain of resource-processing, characterized by the extreme development of human specialist knowledge, and hence of 'specialists'. The result of this is that the majority of lay-people in the industrialized world are effectively unaware of how resources that are essential to their survival are actually procured or processed. They are predominantly 'separated' from any involvement with the processing of the resources on which their very survival depends.

In addition to this, and whilst apparently offering to communicate people with people, today's high-tech communication systems in fact allow us to live apart. Instead of our communing on a local, human-scale, these conceptualized systems facilitate communication with people and places 'elsewhere', so that increasingly, we spend our time effectively *separated* from the 'here' in which we actually, ecologically, live.

In this way, we can see that the attempted *separation* of most of humankind from its resource-base, and more recently from the processing of its essential resources, has characterized much of the evolution of today's global economic system.

I hope that this concise presentation of the hypothesized evolution of our current economic system can serve to highlight the fact that all its conceptual components reinforce the need for all its other conceptual components, and that consequently the system is functionally *cohesive*. The reason for this is that once the concept of ownership had taken hold – once humankind began to be effectively *separated* from its resource-base – the need for all subsequent 'economic' concepts was established. In recognition of this fact we can claim that ownership is the conceptual basis upon which today's entire economic system is established. Thus paradoxically today's functionally *cohesive* economic system is founded upon the *divisive* concept of ownership.

Ever heard the dictum: 'Divide and control'? Well, I believe that in having attempted to establish today's economic system, humankind has been trying to do just that to itself.

Our Assumption of Separability

Embodied in its primary concept of ownership, humankind's 'assumption of separability' underpins the whole of its endeavour to create a conceptualized, economic existence for itself. During recent millenia, humankind has assumed that it has been quite acceptable to attempt to separate itself, institutionally and physically, from the Earthly resource-base of which it is a part, and that it would in no way hurt or impoverish itself by attempting so to do. Humankind has also assumed that it has been in order for it to attempt to manage its conceptualized, economic existence in a way which has been effectively separated from any acknowledgement of the qualities of functioning that characterize Nature, and as part of it, humankind as well.

What is more, intrinsic in the conceptualized, economic management of its existence has been the notion that humankind can do a better job than Nature in providing a pleasant living of life. 'If we will only sufficiently analyse and manipulate the ecosystems around us, then we can all aspire to a 'better living' of life than the one we have at the moment'. It's as if we have accepted, on the basis of the assumption of separability, that there is an 'additional volume', an 'additional existence' over and above the one we are in at the moment, to which we can all aspire if only we will make the conceptualized effort to get into it.

However, our ecologically cohesive context does not permit such an additional, separate existence. This existence, in view of its absolute cohesion, is the only one there can be – and we are part of it.

During an informal discussion in 1911, Harry Snodgrass is reported as having said: 'There's no room for gaps in a cohesive reality'. In so saying, he was attempting to dispel the notion that 'separability' might in fact be a problem in humankind's attemptedly conceptualized living of life.

In this cohesive reality, there *is no* separability, and therefore separability cannot be our problem. Rather, it is our *assumption* that things can be separate that is deserving of our attention. For if there is anything which is spoiling the atmosphere in which we experience our existence it is, I believe, our *assumption* that separation is possible. The entirety, not just of the human family, but of all existence is wronged by the assumption of its separability.

Nonetheless, in having attempted to conceptualize the whole of its own and its environment's existence, humankind has had to assume that a separation from its existence has been possible. Ultimately, therefore, humankind has effectively created for itself an all-pervasive conceptualized atmosphere, within which it has to make its every move and from which it must take its every breath. And this conceptualized atmosphere is inevitably totally infused with the *assumption of separability*: nuclear waste disposal systems; the assumed separation of means from ends, for example military violence to achieve peace; a mammalian humankind bottle-feeding its children. It is *this* that is souring not only humankind's relationship with its Earthly and universal environment, but also its relationship with itself.

Thus, as I said earlier, as a result of its attempt to pursue a conceptualized economic existence, the whole of the human family has been polarised into apparently opposing and conflicting groups, which is why we find ourselves referring to:

the owning minority	the resourceless majority
North	South
developed	underdeveloped
employers	employees
lay-person	specialist

All these are examples of apparently separately identifiable groups of the human family, and as we draw towards the conclusion of this conceptualized discussion, which is itself inevitably based upon the assumption of separability, there is, as a consequence, a tremendously powerful inclination to be *critical* of one or other of these separately identifiable groups, as being perhaps predominantly responsible for the predicament in which humankind now finds itself.

162

Thus, for example, the resourceless majority could easily be critical of the owning minority, or people on the 'loss' side of the economic equation could easily be critical of those on the 'profit' side of the same equation, etc. However, I honestly believe such criticism is not ecologically valid.

This is because 'criticism' is itself founded upon its own version of the assumption of separability, since intrinsic in the act of identifying an entity or group to criticize, is the inference that that entity or group is in some way the main or even the sole cause of a generally unfavourable situation. In this way, a separability of blame is manifested. But we are not dealing with something that has been 'done' by one party or one group, to another. Rather, in considering humankind's long-term attempt to conceptualize and to create a conceptualized existence for itself, we are looking at an endeavour that *all* of us are attempting to do, to *all* of us; and in considering economics we are looking at a supposed 'concept' that *all* of us are trying to make *all* of us conform to. Consequently, we cannot be concerned with criticizing the activities of one group or another, nor of bringing one recalcitrant group or another into line. Rather, I feel, we are *all* involved in attempting to *let go* of something that *all* of us are trying to do to *all* of us.

A Global Economic Totalitarianism

The most widespread manifestation of the global economic system's assumption of separability is represented in its attempt to separate most of humankind from its resource-base. Today, the majority of humankind has had the majority of its resource-base 'owned away' from it. Thus, for example, as we saw earlier, it is estimated that 75 per cent of all the land in the world that can be owned, is controlled by 2.5 per cent of the world's land- owners (see p 64). In most countries of the world the majority of the human population does not have uncontested access to the resource-base upon which it depends for its very survival, and of which it is a part. Its only means of access is *via* the economic system, which effectively makes the economic system a totalitarianism.

163

If I consider my own situation, I find that since my lifelong ambition has been to gain access to perhaps one acre of land, upon which to work in as ecologically harmonious a way as possible, to provide a sufficiency of resources for my family's wellbeing, I can only gain that access, anywhere in the world, *through* the global economic system. I have to own the land or rent it from a landowner, which is an acknowledgement of the principle of ownership; however I don't want to 'own' a resource, I just want to 'use' it, and work on it, to satisfy my ecological needs. Once I begin to buy resources, as I am forced to do, I have to get embroiled in the market economy and all its financial and technical imperatives, in order to maximize my economic advantage. Other than by going *via* the economic system, there isn't one acre for me to 'use', anywhere. The economic system hasn't left any: it's taken them *all*. It's a totalitarianism.

Recently I read of another example of this point in the *Guardian* newspaper. The Innu Indians of Canada were here in England to launch a campaign to stop Nato from siting its largest tactical weapons training-centre at Goosebay, Labrador, Canada. These Indians still hunt and gather in that region; they are not demanding overmuch from the Earth's resource-base, and what is more, they are satisfied with the little they have. The United States and the Nato allies, however, who have such an over-plentitude of resources and function at a level way past ecological sufficiency, want *more*. They want to take Goose Bay from these quiet people. Sufficiency is not enough for the US and Nato, and the economic system of which they are a part. They want *every* square mile of the North American continent. They are part of a totalitarian system.

Addressing the government commissioners at Warner's Hot Springs at the turn of the century, Cecilio Blacktooth speaks about why her people would not surrender their land:

We thank your for coming here to talk to us in a way we can understand. It is the first time anyone has done so. You ask us to think what place we like next best to this place, where we always lived. You see the graveyard out there? There are our fathers and our grandfathers. You see that Eagle-nest mountain and that Rabbit-hole mountain? When God made them, He gave us this place. We have always been here. We do not care for any other place...We have always lived here. We would rather die here. Our fathers did. We cannot leave them. Our children were born here – How can we go away? If you give us the best place in the world, it is not so good for us as this...This is our home...We cannot live anywhere else. We were born here and our fathers are buried here...We want this place and not any other...

There is no other place for us. We do not want you to buy any other place for us. If you will...buy this place, we will go into the mountains like quail, and die there, the old people, and the women and children. Let the Government be glad and proud. It can kill us. We do not fight. We do what it says. If we cannot live here, we want to go into the mountains and die. We do not want any other home.

An excerpt from *Touch the Earth*, 1971,
edited by T.C. McLuhan.

Another incident indicative of the absolute hold economics and the economic system has over the entirety of our resource-base hit the British headlines in the summer of 1986 when a group of so-called 'hippies' assembled in southern England. Essentially, or so at least it seemed to me, they didn't simply wish to denigrate the society into which they were born. They did reject its ethics but manifested that rejection by trying to live their lives in a way which was nearer to their own ethical stance. But where could they go, geographically, to do this? In our industrialized, commercialized society we are *all* asked to accept absolutely its socio-economic concepts and philosophy; we are *all* asked to conform, for example, to our society's laws of ownership and of financial exchange, etc.

The 'hippies' didn't *want* to draw dole-money and to be enforced 'hangers-on' to the consumer society they abhored. What they wanted, I believe, was 'resources', mainly land, on which they could live and rest, work, and generate the essential resources for their own sustenance. 'Well', some might retort, 'all they had to do was get off their back-sides, work hard, save their wages and buy some land. Then they would have had the resources they wanted.' And I would say to that proposition: 'Exactly'.

That process would require them to commit their lifetime's work to the absolute dictates of ownership, employment and financial exchange etc. It's a totalitiarianism.

For my own part, I want to be satisified and content with the energy, beauty and resources that Nature provides. But to be thus satisfied and content, I have to have access to those things. I have to have access to them, so that I can put my own energy into them and thereby extract the resources that I need from them. But in order for me to gain such access, so that I can be 'satisfied with Nature', I have to commit a lifetime's work to the 'dissatisfied with Nature' system. I have to work through this system for all my useful working life, to gain access to the resources that Nature is giving me anyway. I can only obtain such access by going through the economic system that is effectively, absolutely interposed between me and the Nature of which I am a part. Why? Because today's economic system is a global totalitarianism.

In being a *true* totalitarianism, today's economic system applies itself with equal absoluteness to those at the supposed 'top' of our socio-economic hierarchies as to those at the 'bottom'. Thus, in attempting to reduce the current US budget deficit, for example, even the President of the United States of America has to make obeisance to the dictates of the economic system. This observation is important in that it allows us to recognize, once again, that it is not the people at the supposed 'top' of our economic societies who are applying a totalitarian economic rule to those at the 'bottom'. Rather, it is a totalitarianism that *all* of us are attempting to apply to *all* of us.

This was recently well illustrated in an advert by a large company, which featured a picture of the Earth taken from space with a caption that implied that its clientele was the whole world. It makes you wonder just where the company's head office is situated.

Untitled (I shop therefore I am) 1987, by Barbara Kruger; by kind permission of the artist.
– a consumer-side view of today's totalitarian, economic situation.

Uniformity, Diversity and Ecological Sustainability

In an ecologically cohesive reality, humankind's totalitarian attempt to separate itself from its resource-base is bad enough in its own right, but when we also take into account the system's efforts to instil imbalance into an ecologically self-balancing reality, and perpetual acceleration into an ecologically paced reality (in the forms of the profit-motive and economic growth), then a question-mark is raised over how long today's economic system can keep itself going.

It is as an inbuilt, automatic response to this uncertainty, I believe, that the economic system has evolved into a global totalitarianism, because in having so become, it perhaps feels itself better set to *enforce* its economic dictates upon an inexorably ecological humankind, and an irrefutably ecological Earthly environment.

But in having thus evolved, the resultant totalitariansim is, in reality, endangering its own sustainability. This is because of the degree of conformity, and hence *uniformity* it is insisting upon, in what is ultimately an ecologically *diverse* world.

The evolution of any totalitarian system necessarily involves the attempt to make people and ecosystems conform to its rules and criteria. Whilst in their embryonic form, these rules and criteria might well be diverse, as the system matures and takes firmer hold they are inevitably standardized and move in the general direction of increased *uniformity*. For example, thousands of years ago there existed innumerable, diverse 'barter' systems, in which many different resources were exchanged one for another; whereas today, 'monetarised' systems of exchange account for the vast majority of the world's trade in commodities and products. Similarly, hundreds of years ago, a very wide diversity of food products at an almost infinitely variable range of 'prices' fed the world's human population, whereas today a handful of staple foods with globally acknowledged world-market prices feeds a major proportion of the world's 5 billion people.

A totalitarian system fosters uniformity in what, in retrospect, can be seen to be its drive for ascendancy and control.

This is because wherever commodities, prices, methodologies, etc. can be made the same or similar, there lies the potential for standardized norm-setting, by which the movement of resources can be monitored and hence controlled.

However, this same evolution towards economic unformity also necessarily generates a trend towards an attempted ecological standardization, when one of the great qualities which ecological evolution displays is its tendency towards diversity and complexity. For example, over the last few thousand years a very large number of different wheat, barley and oat varieties have been consumed by humankind in the temperate zones, as staple foods. Today, however, an ever smaller number of varieties account for a large proportion of grain tonnages consumed, and most of them are grown in monoculture syustems. Similarly, whereas 300 years ago there were literally thousands of different types of agriculture practised around the world, each having evolved to suit its own particular niche, in the last hundred years there has been a large-scale endeavour to introduce broadly 'westernized' models of agriculture to areas that are climatically, topographically and vegetatively different to the temperate areas of the world. (See, for example, *Beyond the Green Revolution* 1979, by K. Dahlberg.) Again on a global scale, the energy-systems previously employed by indigenous peoples on the various continents of the world – wood, draught animals, water, fire, wind, etc. – all varied enormously, whereas today, the global, economy-driven, standardized trend is inexorably towards higher levels of energy consumption and towards systems producing electricity.

'So what?' you might well ask, in a fit of spontaneous disinterest. Well, ecological complexity and its infinite *diversity* of form are critical factors in the establishment of ecological sustainability; and that is something that is of relevance to all of us.

The diversity of shape, texture, consistency, physical state, rate, proportion, etc. allows the components of an ecosystem to interlink, interact, interlock and hence to cohere. The convex coheres with the concave, the hard with the soft, the animal interacts with the vegetable, the male with the female; the organic interacts with the inorganic and the wet is taken-up by the dry, etc. Therefore, any attempt to reduce diversity must begin to undermine that system's cohesive capability and, consequently, its ecological sustainability.

As depicted earlier (see page 135), an ecosystem's functioning involves the receipt, cycling and eventual loss of Universal energy – be it a plant, my body, a rainforest canopy, an atom, or the Earth's entire ecosystem. Where the pathway which the energy follows is straightforward and simple, and where its cycling is uninterrupted, it can leave the system quickly. But if the pathway it has to follow is convoluted, complex and circuitous, with loop-backs and cycles within cycles, then that pathway inevitably becomes 'extended'. The energy, therefore, remains in that system for a relatively longer time. That is, where the pathway the energy has to follow involves transfers between many diverse forms of matter/energy and between many, diverse sub-ecosystems, then that ecosystem's sustainability is enhanced.

For example, the ecology of the Moon's surface is much more simple, less diverse and less complex than that on Earth, and as a result, incoming solar energy is bounced back off its surface ecosystem much more quickly than on Earth. Here on Earth incoming solar energy that is incident upon a rainforest canopy might remain in the Earth's ecosystem for millions of years, first as vegetation, then as decomposed vegetation, then as fossilized vegetation, coal and oil. This means that we can assert that an ecosystem's ecological sustainability is enhanced by its diversity and complexity.

But as we noted earlier, today's economic totalitariansism is fostering not only economic uniformity, but also a process of ecological standardization. Therefore we can conclude that on a global scale the ecological base of our activities is being narrowed, so that the ecological stability and sustainability of the resource-procurement systems on which humankind depends for its survival are being undermined.

In addition, we can note that in a reality which, at its most basic level, is made up of various permutations of energy, the attempt to impose uniformity onto a so-called 'diverse' ecology is effectively an attempt to halt existence's energized evolution.

'Diversity of form' is the conceptualized label given to a series of 'still-photographs' of what is, in reality, 'movement', 'change' or 'mobility'. And this is true, I believe, whatever the time spans involved. If, for example, I raise my arm to drink a pint of beer, and sixteen cine-camera frames capture the action on film, then each one will depict a different position of my arm; a 'diversity' of arm positions will be displayed. Similarly, the emergence of a flower-head from a plant's stem, if photographed at different times during spring and summer, would reveal a 'diversity' in the plant's shape and structure. Equally, a 'diversity' in form and capability is observable during the evolution of land-based animals after their first emergence from the sea. Each separately observed form of land-animal, however, merely represents a fixed point in a continuum of evolutionary change that has gone on for millions of years.

The ecological reality is not the 'snapshot' which gives rise to the notion of diversity; the ecological reality is movement itself; the change, and the motility which constitutes the evolution, and which, in terms of diversity, we can describe as 'energized diversity'. Since, ultimately, existence *is* energy, and since

171

energy can do nothing other than move and change, then 'energized diversity' is an absolutely inevitable characteristic of existence and evolution. So what is ecologically important is not diversity itself, but 'energized diversity' – that is, flexibility, movement, and change.

If, therefore, the attempt to engender uniformity, observable in the workings of today's global economic totalitariansism, is an attempt to counter 'energized diversity', then in ecological reality it represents an endeavour to *stop* existence's movement and hence its very evolution.

Whether we assert that today's economic push towards uniformity represents an attempt to halt evolution in its tracks or to undermine ecological sustainability, either way we can say that its totalitarian efforts are not conducive to improving the chances of its own survival.

Economics Itself is the Problem

The chances for the survival of the ecosystems from which humankind takes its resources is an oft-debated topic in the current discussions on the environment. Concern is frequently expressed, for example, about the physical impact human activity is having on the Earth's tropical rainforest systems; about the extinctions of species resulting from our excessive harvesting of resource-systems; about the human nutritional consequences of severe imbalances in the global distribution of food; and about the impacts our energy-intensive industries and practices are having on the Earth's climatic conditions, etc.

However, whilst such concerns are totally valid, whilst observations at this level desperately need to be made, and whilst reactions to these observations desperately need to be implemented, this is not the level at which our concern can be allowed to rest. At this level we are only referring ourselves to the symptoms of relative ecological malfunction, rather than to their causes. For these, we have to focus our attention on the *framework of economic concepts*, – ownership, exchange, profit, employment, economic growth, etc. – within which *all* of our

172

commercial, social and industrial endeavour is made to function today.

For let it be said that it is **Economics** – that is, the 'consequence' of humankind's attempt to create the concept of economics – that is *causing*, that is *requiring* industry and commerce:

to attempt to accelerate perpetually,

to attempt to introduce imbalance into,

to attempt to impose uniformity onto,

and to attempt to infuse separation throughout the totality of humankind's current activity and living. Industry and commerce are but the handmaidens of Economics.

Economic humankind's attempted perpetual *acceleration*, attempted maintenance of situations of *imbalance*, attempted enforcement of *uniformity*, and attempted insertion of *separation* into the Earth's paced, self-balancing, diverse and cohesive ecosystems are the 'deeper pollutants' of our beautiful world; a world, let us not forget, that includes a humankind whose own ecological sensibility is also deeply affected by the self-same pollutants. And it is Economics that is the fount of this deeper pollution.

Happily, however, none of these human economic endeavours is ecologically sustainable, since diversity, balance, rate and cohesion etc. are eternal, universal qualities which will always, ultimately assert themselves.

Ecology Into Economics Won't Go

We can reinforce the assertion that our attempted, totalitarian, economic management of our living is ecologically unsustainable, by allowing ourselves the time to re-emphasize something that was said in the previous section. 'Economics' is not made out of iron girders – it doesn't need painting each year, nor are there any bolts holding it together – but it *is* a framework. It is a 'conceptual framework' that has accumulated over the millennia as a result of ourcontinuing attempt to instil a conceptualized management into the living of our lives. It is a 'framework of concepts' within which *all* our human endeavour and industry is currently being made to function. Humankind is trying to force the functioning of *all* the Earth's ecosystems, including its own, into the conceptual dictates of this economic framework; it is trying to stuff the *whole* of the Earth's ecology into the concept of economics.

However, as we discussed in some detail at the start of this book, in the ecological existence of which humankind is a part, it is not possible for us to 'conceptualize' in an ecologically meaningful way, because humankind cannot fit the *whole* of ecological existence into its 'concept' of existence. Similarly, therefore, but this time with regard to humankind's current attempt to fit the absolute *entirety* of life here on Earth into the 'concept of economics', we can say that this attempt too is not ecologically possible.

It also follows from our earlier discussions on humankind's long-term attempt to conceptualize, that if humankind cannot conceptualize, if it cannot create 'concepts', then in ecological reality, concepts do not exist, and hence, the 'concept of economics' does not exist. Consequently, if the 'concept' of economics does not exist, then there *is nothing* into which humankind can attempt to stuff its current experience of living.

'Has anybody seen the Concept of Economics?'

174

Therefore, whether we say that in ecological reality there is no 'concept of economics' into which we can try to force all human living, or whether we say it is not possible for us to fit the *absolute entirety* of our lives into the supposed 'concept of economics'...

Either way, we can reasonably agree with what Harry Snodgrass Senior said in 1910 when he concluded that: 'Ecology into economics won't go'. Because you see, he was right.

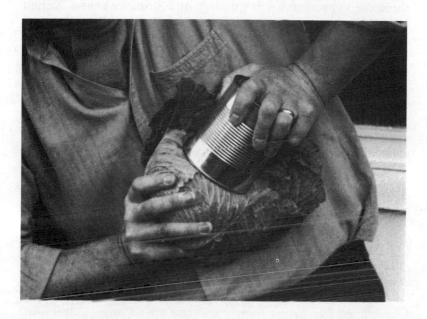

Attempting to Live a Concept of Our Lives

In having attempted to see all existence as a concept, in having attempted to create a conceptualized existence for itself and, more recently, in having attempted to create a conceptualized economic lifestyle for itself, humankind, as we established in our earlier discussions, has been attempting to 'sense-again' the sensibility that *is* its experience of life; it has been trying to

175

'loop-back' on the process of its actual experiencing. It is as though we have been trying to 'be' for a second time, through the instant we've just 'been' through, and though only fractional, the attempt must introduce a sort of 'time-lag', which will be perpetual, if our attempt to conceptualize is perpetual.

In accepting such a time-lag, I think we have perhaps deluded ourselves with regard to the usefulness of the supposed 'awareness' we think it has brought us, because the only timely sensings we have of the stimuli coming to us in our 'now' are those we get through our intuitive and primary senses, which are part of our 'now' experiencing. Our supposed 'awareness' always trails behind.

Thus, in reality, in having tried to make ourselves 'aware', we have condemned ourselves to the living of a perpetuated 'afterthought'. Our supposed 'awareness' has put us one step behind the 'now' in which we actually exist, and as our supposed 'awareness' has increased, we have lagged more and more behind. The 'dumb' animals have never developed an 'awareness' to this extent. They exist in, and fully experience, their 'now', so that they are not one step behind all the time. They have not 'advanced' to the point of attempting to 'loop-back' on their senses, but at least they are alive to the 'now' in which they actually exist. Animals 'feel' with their senses, they don't try to 'think' with a mind; they are sensible of their actual, immediate 'now', not aware of a 'then' that has already gone past.

Similarly, from birth, our children have an absolutely full complement of primary senses and an overall, intuitive ability to feel and sense the immediacy of their real 'now' existence. Our babies live in the 'now', and the speed and precision of their sensibilities often surprise adults. That we *are* surprised is testimony to the extent to which we adults have allowed a conceptualized view of life to form a sort of 'crust' over our own primary ability to sense and feel.

Several aboriginal peoples still existing today have somehow managed to avoid the process of attempted conceptualization getting to an extreme such that it all but obscures their real intuitive sensing of their 'now' existence. Such peoples have certainly made the attempt to conceptualize, as we have done in the 'developed' world, but the attempt has not been allowed to go to the point where an effective *dislocation* from the real intuitive sensing of their 'now' experience is created.

I feel that for them, their intuitive sensibility and intuitive responding are accepted as the stuff of their actual existing. It is from this that they derive their reverence for everything in their experience of their environments. (See, for example, *The Forest People*, 1961, by Colin Turnbull.) This reverence is a manifestation of their acceptance of the fact that they are an intrinsic *part of* their creation and environment; not above it, not below it, just part of it. It is a manifestation of their acceptance of the need to remain true to their real ecological sensibility, and hence to remain intuitively sensible of their actual ecological 'now'. Another browse through the lovely anthology entitled *Touch the Earth* by T.C. McLuhan gives ample and rich evidence of this sensibility.

Ohiyesa, the celebrated writer, looks back over the past:

As a child I understood how to give; I have forgotten this grace since I became civilized. I lived the natural life, whereas I now live the artificial. Any pretty pebble was valuable to me. Then every growing tree an object of reverence. Now I worship with the white man before a painted landscape whose value is estimated in dollars. Thus the Indian is reconstructed, as the natural rocks are ground to powder and made into artificial blocks which may be built into the walls of modern society.

The first American mingled with his pride a singular humility. Spiritual arrogance was foreign to his nature and teaching. He never claimed that the power of articulate speech was proof of superiority over the dumb creation; on the other hand, it is to him a perilous gift. He believes profoundly in silence – the sign of a perfect equilibrium. Silence is the absolute poise or balance of body, mind and spirit. The man who preserves his selfhood is ever calm and unshaken by the storms of existence – not a leaf, as it were, astir on the tree; not a ripple upon the surface of the shining pool – his, in the mind of the unlettered sage, is the ideal attitude and conduct of life.

If you ask him, 'What is silence' he will answer: 'It is the Great Mystery.' 'The holy silence is His voice!' If you ask: 'What are the fruits of silence?' he will say: 'They are self-control, true

courage or endurance, patience, dignity, and reverence. Silence is
the cornerstone of character.'

Every shaman, an Indian holy man, has his own particular
song which he sings when calling up his helping spirits. This
was the song of Uvavnuk, an Eskimo woman shaman, celebrat-
ing the joy of being moved by nature. 'To the Indian', writes
Natalie Curtis in *The Indian's Book*, 'song is the breath of the
spirit that consecrates the act of life.':

> The great sea
> Has sent me adrift
> It moves me
> As the weed in a great river
> Earth and the great weather
> Move me
> Have carried me away
> And move my inward parts with joy.

And elsewhere in the same anthology:

> We love quiet; we suffer the mouse to play; when
> the woods are rustled by the wind, we fear not.

Indian Chief to the governor
of Pennsylvania, 1796

Such aboriginal peoples have not allowed their own attempts
to conceptualize to go so far as to separate them from their
sensing of the natural world. Thus their wisdom is said to
emanate *from* the animals, trees, forest and rocks; it comes out
of Nature to them. It does not come from themselves, back to
themselves, and hence there is not the same danger of an
effective 'looping-back, 'budding-off' or *separation* from the
real ecological existence of which they are a part. For example:

> The occasion for this speech was an Indian council in the Valley of
> Walla Walla in 1855, presided over by Isaac Stevens, governor of
> Washington Territory, and General Palmer, superintendent of In-
> dian Affairs for Oregon. Governor Steven's objectives were to set
> up three reservations: one for the Cayuses, the Walla-Wallas and
> Umatillas; a second for the Nez Perces; and a third for the Yakimas.

Young Chief, of the Cayuses, opposed the treaty and grounded his objections on the fact that the Indians had no right to sell the ground which the Great Spirit had given for their support. He gave the following speech before signing away their land.

'I wonder if the ground has anything to say? I wonder if the ground is listening to what is said? I wonder if the ground would come alive and what is on it? Though I hear what the ground says. The ground says, it is the Great Spirit that placed me here. The Great Spirit tells me to take care of the Indians, to feed them aright. The Great Spirit appointed the roots to feed the Indians on. The water says the same thing, The Great Spirit directs me, Feed the Indians well. The grass says the same thing, Feed the Indians well. The ground, water and grass say, The Great Spirit has given us our names. We have these names and hold these names. The ground says, The Great Spirit has placed me here to produce all that grows on me, trees and fruit. The same way the ground says, it was from me man was made. The Great Spirit, in placing men on the earth, desired them to take good care of the ground and to do each other no harm...'

Two Strike, of the Brulé tribe

(from *Touch the Earth*, 1971, by T.C. McLuhan)

In the film *Little Big Man*, a story is told which depicts a white American child's adoption and upbringing by a North American Indian tribe. As a teenager, the boy asks his Indian foster grandfather whether the severing of his grandfather's optic-nerve in a battle with the US cavalry has rendered him blind. 'No', says the Indian grandfather, 'like the white man, my eyes can see, but my heart can't feel'. He is saying, I believe, that his eyes, like the white man's, have effectively been *separated* from the centre of his sensibilities, with the result that his eyes still take in light rays, but he doesn't *sense* them.

In the same way, I feel that today, whilst our intuitive 'being' is still inevitably part of our real ecological 'now', and whilst our intuitions are therefore fully sensible of the stimuli coming in from our real, ecological 'here', we are not allowing ourselves to feel and experience that real intuitive sensing. This is because our supposedly conceptualized version of experiencing currently predominates, and this effectively subjugates our intuition and cuts us off from being intuitively sensible of our situation.

Conceptualizing humankind, in supposing that it has become 'aware', has effectively severed itself from any real sensing of the real 'now' in which it really exists. Conceptualizing humankind doesn't respond to reality anymore, because that happens 'now', and by the time it has managed to think about it, that bit of reality has already gone past.

For my own part, my feeling is of a repression or of an effective denial of what I really 'feel' to be the case inside; an attempted separation from my internal, unstoppable feelings, that are already there as a result of my spontaneous, intuitive sensing of my immediate situation. For example:

- I continue in polite conversation, whilst feeling perhaps deeply hurt inside if someone is dealing with me in an arrogant way.
- I might do something which is convenient for my own conceptualized purposes, but which I feel inside will cause hurt and upset to someone else.
- If I am relaxing, whilst bathed in the warmth of the sun, and can feel the colour and the warmth doing me good, I

might then make myself get up and 'do another job', out of a conceptualized sense of duty.

- I might sense inside that I am good at a certain activity and that that activity 'is for me'; but nonetheless, still make myself engage in another activity or profession that is perhaps held in higher social esteem.
- I might be politely friendly with someone, when in fact they 'get on my nerves'; or conversely, I might really like and admire someone, but not be able to express my feelings because of some social stricture, or because it is not 'seemly' to do so.
- I might feel absolutely tired, body and soul, but still make myself get up to go to work at seven o'clock, or go to a party or a meeting, instead of doing what I feel my whole being is telling me to do; namely, go to bed and sleep.

A lot of supposedly conceptualizing human beings spend a lot of their time and a lot of their nervous energy making themselves accept what they think they have to accept, rather than doing what they *feel* intuitively would be wholesome and beneficial for them to do.

How many conceptualizing human beings in the so-called 'developed' countries of the world, are today, a Tuesday, actually doing what they feel they would really be content to be doing, or even what they feel they need to be doing; rather than merely fulfilling the conceptualized function they find themselves slotted into? How many of us, the world's conceptualizing human beings, feel today that we would like to be in some predicament other than that in which we actually are? Or that we would like to be engaged in a type of activity in which we could treat other people differently to the way in which we seem to have to treat them? Or that we would like to use the resources around us in a qualitatively and quantitatively different way to the way in which we are having to use them?

If the answer to these questions is 'A lot of us', then this suggests to me, at a supposedly conceptualized level, that a lot of us need to put effort into getting into that other predicament; we need to apply ourselves mentally and physically, perhaps for most of a lifetime, to make sure we 'get ourselves into' this preferred situation, so that we could then live in the way our 'feelings' and 'sensings' would have us live. *But in this I would be wrong.*

In the fact that 'feelings' and our 'intuitive sensings' constitute our here and now existence, we are already *a part of* the existence we strive after. We don't need to make efforts to 'be' anywhere else; all we need to do is allow ourselves to feel what we are already feeling here and now. These feelings are the mobilizers and the moulders that can engender and ensure our ecological survival, satisfaction and contentment 'here'; these intuitive sensings are the drives and direction-indicators that bring us into an ecological harmony with ourselves, all human beings, and with all other ecological entities, because we are all part of the one same sensibility.

But paradoxically, what is precluding us from being 'in' this harmonious existence, what is effectively stopping us from experiencing what we actually *are,* is our very attempt to 'be' in a different existence. The very attempt we make, to live in a conceptualized realm of reality, effectively takes us out of, extracts us from our real, intuitive, sensible, 'here and now' existing. It sucks us out of the *immediacy* of our actual experience of life.

The *effort* we make to find for ourselves, and to climb into, another supposedly separate, conceptualized realm of existence, in which life is expected to be better than the one we are in at the moment, effectively hoists us out of the ecological sensing that *is* our existence. It is our effort to 'be' somewhere else that effectively separates us from 'being' where we *are.* Thus what we are actually intuitively experiencing today is the sensation that we have become effectively *separated* from the flowing of the feelings and the sensings that make up our ecological experience of life, and hence that we have become effectively *separated* from our ecologically sensible existence.

Paradise, Lost?

Several million years ago, everything that had been ecologically essential for the evolution of humankind up to that point was in fact to hand and available in plentitude. This assertion is based on the simple fact that had it *not* been, humankind would not have evolved up to that point in the way that it had. This is not an expression of nostalgia for a long-lost Paradise; ecologically this must have been the case. That we have labelled such a situation, in retrospect, a 'Paradise Lost' – that is, a situation of unattainable perfection – is not so much an evaluation of its ecological feasibility, but more a manifestation of our effective dislocation from ecological reality.

Such a 'paradisic' state, in which the evolutionary ecological environment provided everything which facilitated a given evolutionary step, must have been the situation throughout evolutionary time. In it, the evolutionary environment provided a range of resources, situations and energies which permitted the subsequent, evolutionary step to be made. Had those resources and energies *not* been available, then quite simply that next evolutionary step would *not* have been made.

Thus what was actually happening in the 'time' of all those millions of years ago was that there was a simultaneous 'blending' of two influences: the 'environment' influenced the 'evolutionary step', and the 'evolutionary step' influenced the 'environment'. And what this now leads us on to recognize is that there was a perfect fit between, and a mutual sensing by, these two evolving influences. In fact, there could not have been anything other than a mutual sensing, because both influences were part of one and the same ecological sensibility – namely, ecological existence and hence, ecological evolution.

And I believe that a fully 'sensing', absolutely *intuitive* group of hominids was part of this ecologically sensible evolution. It was as part of just such an evolutionary, ecologically sensible 'Paradise' and it was as an interwoven thread of just such a cohesive 'paradisic tapestry' that an intuitively sensible humankind existed. Humankind's very existence, all those hundreds of thousands of years ago, was made up of, was

183

composed of, its intuitive and primary sensings. Its sensing capability, and hence its sensibility, constituted the entirety of that which it was.

How and when, therefore, was this evolutionary situation, this ecologically sensible 'Paradise', lost? Or more meaningfully, I think, how and when did an intuitively sensible humankind become effectively lost from or separated from this ecologically sensible 'Paradise'? Well, I think that humankind, or at least a part of it, began to *think itself effectively lost* from this Paradise when it started its attempt to become a conceptualizing, rather than an intuitive humankind.

Happily, however, and as I hope this book has at least started to show, we have never succeeded in this attempt. We have never been able to completely stand back from the sensings of our situation, because those sensings actually make us what we are; we have never been able to completely separate ourselves from our intuitive sensibility, because that sensibility constitutes our very existence; we have never been able to make ourselves anything other than intuitively sensible human beings because we are part of an absolutely cohesive, ecologically sensible evolution.

An intuitively sensible humankind can never be 'lost' from the infinitely cohesive, ecologically sensible 'Paradise' of which it is a part. 'Paradise' is not lost, it is here; and an intuitive humankind is part of it.

Therefore, and with all love and due respect to the singer Joni Mitchell, we can say:

'We are, everyone of us,
part of the garden.'

Chapter Four

Intuitive 'Being'

I NOW THEREFORE WANT TO DEPICT how an intuitively sensible humankind, and indeed, even an attemptedly conceptualizing humankind, is part of this ecologically sensible 'Paradise'; and how humankind *coheres* with ecological existence.

In order to do this I shall have to use words; but words, in being conceptualized, are themselves the products of assumed separability. How, therefore, can I meaningfully use words to achieve this depiction? How can I possibly use the products of *assumed separability* to depict *cohesion*? How can I possibly use conceptualized words to say that nothing can be lost from an absolutely cohesive reality? How can I possibly use conceptualized words to say that an intuitively sensible humankind, even one that assumes that separability is possible and is attempting to conceptualize on that basis; that even such an humankind cannot be separated from, nor lost from an absolutely cohesive, ecologically sensible existence?

Well, I'm afraid I can't. It's not that I'm at a loss for words, it's that my use of 'words' is synonymous with my being 'lost'; effectively lost, that is, from the world of human intuitive 'being'.

Lao Tzu, a contemporary of Confucius, said essentially the same thing, I believe, when, 2400 years ago, he said:

'The Tao that can be spoken of
    is not the constant way'
                                    (from the *Tao Te Ching*, by Lao Tzu,
                                    Book I, verse I, p.57.)

189

And some seventy-nine years ago, Harry Snodgrass Senior demonstrated that he had himself appreciated this point when, whilst eating a banana-split, he said:

> *The only way to depict*
> *the absolute cohesion*
> *between an intuitive humankind*
> *and an ecologically sensible existence*
> *is to shut up.'*
>
> From *A Good Argument for Silence,*
> Harry Snodgrass Senior, 1910.

The full relish of my ecological quality is not available amongst the two-sided vocabulary of a conceptualized description, nor amongst the two-sided unrealities of a conceptualized existence. It flourishes instead, amidst an intuitive living of the curves and proportions, the ebbs and the flows, the cycles and the fluxes, etc., which are intrinsic to the ecology of which I am a part. It flourishes amidst an intuitive celebration of my being ecological:

– of my being part of existence's cohesion,

– of my being paced, according to its rate,

– of my being centred in its balance,

– of my being unique in its diversity,

– and of my being content with its sufficiency.

Quite simply, therefore, it involves me in 'being' what I 'am'.

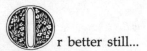r better still...

Two crocodiles are swimming up the Nile, when one says to the other:
'Funny, I keep thinking it's Tuesday.'

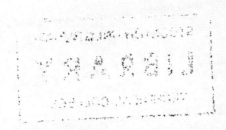